To Mr

From UVK '79

1972

£3-60p

HERBS, SALADS AND TOMATOES

HERBS, SALADS AND TOMATOES

by

W. E. SHEWELL-COOPER

M.B.E., N.D.H., F.L.S., F.R.S.L., Dip. Hort. (Wye), D.Litt.
Commendeur du Mérite Agricole (France)
Knight of Merit (Italy)
Fellow and Doctor of The Horticultural College (Vienna Univ.)
Director, The International Horticultural Advisory Bureau
Lately Command Horticultural Officer, S.E. and E. Commands
Sometime Horticultural Superintendent, Swanley Horticultural College
Horticultural Adviser, Warwickshire and Cheshire County Councils and
Garden Editor, B.B.C. North Region
Hon. Director, The Good Gardeners' Association.

JOHN GIFFORD LTD.
LONDON

First published 1961
This revised edition published 1972
by
John Gifford Ltd.,
125 Charing Cross Road,
London WC2H 0EB.

Copyright © 1961
W. E. Shewell-Cooper

PRINTED IN GREAT BRITAIN BY
BRISTOL TYPESETTING CO. LTD.,
BARTON MANOR - ST. PHILIPS
BRISTOL

DEDICATION
to
The Right Hon. the Lord Luke
President
of
The Good Gardeners' Association

AUTHOR'S PREFACE

I HAVE always been grateful to my father and mother for causing me to learn French conversationally from my babyhood upwards; it has enabled me to be at home in France, a country in which I have spent a great deal of time. Undoubtedly the French are the world's best salad makers and they have brought the use of herbs to a fine art.

Many more people today travel to the continent than ever before, with the result that they in their turn want to fill the salad bowl with all kinds of crops and thus to give the salad at home the piquancy which it had in the favourite restaurant in, say, Normandy.

Not only have I tried to bring my continental experience to bear on the book but, in addition, we have been able in the experimental gardens of The Good Gardeners' Association – to try out various methods of growing herbs and salads as well as to grow the many different varieties available to see which are the most suitable for eating raw.

More and more people are interested in slimming diets and salads are an excellent way of helping to lose 'avoirdupois.' This book, therefore, is designed to show how the numerous crops that can be eaten raw may be grown; while in addition useful hints and tips are given as to their preparation and use on the table.

I am indebted to Miss Gweneth Wood, Dip. Hort. (Swanley), (now Mrs. Roy Johnson), who is on the Council of The Good Gardeners' Association, for her help in going through the script.

My thanks, also, must go to my personal secretary, for so carefully typing all the script.

W. E. SHEWELL-COOPER, Director.

The International Horticultural Advisory Bureau,
    Arkley, Herts.

CONTENTS

	Author's Preface	7
I.	The Soil—Quality, Flavour and Composting	11
II.	Preparing, Planting and Protecting	22
III.	The Use of Cloches	35
IV.	The Use of Dutch Lights and Frames	41
V.	The Growing of Herbs	50
VI.	The Preparation and Drying of Herbs	76
VII.	The Cabbage Family as Salads	82
VIII.	Peas and Beans as Salads	96
IX.	Root Crops as Salads	104
X.	Leaf Crops as Salads	116
XI.	The Bulb Salads	132
XII.	Various Types of Celery	140
XIII.	Cucumbers	147
XIV.	The Tomato Story	155
XV.	Tomatoes in the Open	158
XVI.	Tomatoes Under Glass	167
XVII.	Tomatoes Under Ganwicks	189
XVIII.	Tomatoes and Ring Culture	204
XIX.	A Few Simple Recipes	209
XX.	Seed Sowing and Tomatoes	213
	Appendix	215

CHAPTER I

THE SOIL – QUALITY, FLAVOUR AND COMPOSTING

ONE of the things which distresses the keen salad lover is the fact that so many of the crops that he sees available in the greengrocers' shops have apparently lost not only in vitamin quality but also in the true old-fashioned flavour. The cutting of a lettuce in Hampshire – its depatch to London in a polythene bag; its primary sale (maybe) in Covent Garden, leads to its display in a local shop, where it may stay for a few days before reaching a home. There is naturally all the difference between this rather flaccid plastic-covered lettuce and the gloriously fresh specimen cut from one's own compost garden under ideal conditions.

It may be possible to disguise, or even to pretend to forget flavour, when a vegetable is boiled or steamed, but you always get the truth 'in the raw' when you prepare the salad bowl. Here, every salading must be crisp and fresh and it is flavour which counts every time. Does this flavour come from the variety grown, or does it emanate in the first place from the soil in which its roots have had their being?

Dr. R. F. Milton has been able to show at the Haughley Research Station in Suffolk that it is 'quality' that counts every time; the cows, for instance, fed on food from the organically manured section of the farm have consistently given more and better milk, from *less* actual food, than from similar cows fed with greater bulk from the sections of the farm which were given a chemical fertiliser. What matters, therefore, it seems is quality and not quantity, and quality comes from soil in the right condition.

In the good old days gardeners were able to get hold of large quantities of farmyard manure to dig in every winter; they never thought of using artificial chemical fertilisers for they knew nothing about them. It was by the regular addition of *well rotted*

VARIOUS WAYS IN WHICH PLANT FOODS ARE LOST

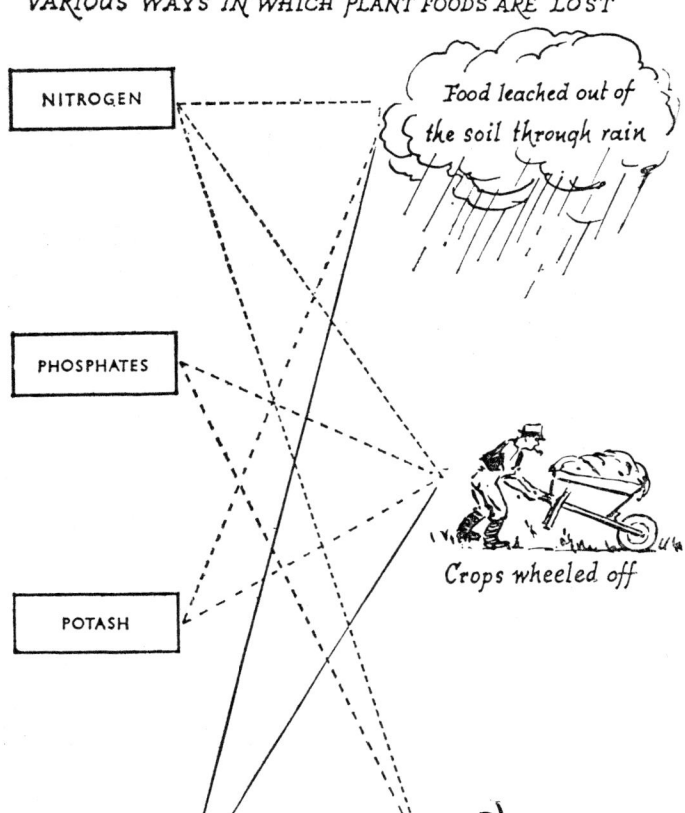

animal manure that the soil was kept in a high state of fertility. It was not only because these manures contained certain 'salt solutions' which fed the plants, but because of the humus-forming material that such manure produced.

Unfortunately the term humus has been used to represent any organic matter whether it is well rotted or even in a fresh state.

Surely humus should only refer to the brown or black jelly-like substance in the soil itself, which has been called its 'life colloid', A Yorkshireman cannot actually point to the fresh egg in his Yorkshire pudding but he can soon tell whether it is there or not. He rightly resents the so-called Yorkshire pudding produced with dried ersatz egg powder.

An efficient gardener knows that a good soil must be of the right texture and that this texture and the surface tilth, in which the seeds are sown – can only be produced if the recipe is complete. There must be the particles of rock, the fine deposits of clay or sand, the jelly-like humus, a little lime and so on; just as there must be eggs and flour and sugar and, of course, fat of some sort, in a delicious cake. Each ingredient in the cake has some part to play, as has each ingredient in the soil. The jelly-like humus holds the water and the plant foods, as well as helping to improve the tilth. The slightly less rotten vegetable material helps to keep the soil open and workable, the grains of granite, limestone or sand give the soil stability and strength and the roots of the plants thus delight in the perfect soil recipe produced for them.

So keen are the French salad growers on organic matter and humus that the market gardeners around Paris use as much as 500 tons of manure per acre each year and when I say 500 tons, I really do mean 500 tons. Many market gardeners in Great Britain think they have done wonders if they work in 30 tons an acre! These French *maraîchers* are able, as a result of regular applications of organic matter over a series of years—to take six or seven crops off the same piece of soil in any one season. It is no exaggeration to say that each salad produced on such land is very delicious, full of flavour, and of very high vitamin quality.

THE LIVING ORGANISMS

Up to now nothing has been said of the living organisms in the soil; the soil in fact is alive with millions of 'citizens' which cannot be seen without the aid of a microscope. In fact, when I hold in my hand a handful of good soil it can easily contain 28,000,000 living organisms which, if given the right conditions, will work morning, noon and night for the benefit of mankind.

They work on the organic matter dug or forked into the soil and convert it into the jelly-like humus already described.

Certain scientists, and particularly chemists, have suggested that plants can be given the food they need in a purely chemical form. During the last twenty years there has been a tremendous spate of advertising in the press in respect of these artificial chemical foods and in consequence of which they are being used in greater and greater quantities. This may well be one of the factors that is leading to a lack of quality and flavour.

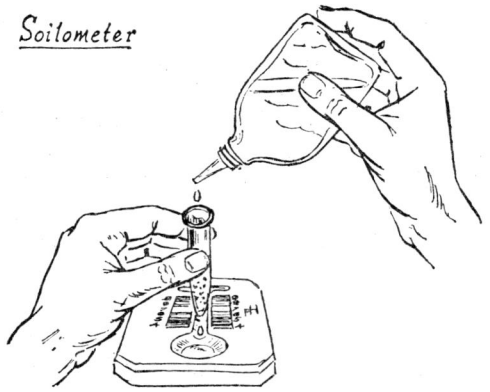

Testing the soil for acidity finding out the pH.

It has been assumed in the past that chemical fertilisers are plant foods, as claimed by the manufacturers, that is to say that the minerals they contain are taken up and used by the plants. The Haughley Research Station on the other hand has shown that the plants on the section of the farm whose soil is fed only with organic matter and is never given any chemical fertilisers at all – take up as much, and more, as the plants on the other sections, despite all the chemical fertilisers these are given. May not this mean that the utilisation of minerals by plants and the action of fertilisers, may be very different indeed from what has hitherto been supposed?

When dealing with soil, the bacteria or living organisms must never be forgotten. They must be given the right conditions so that they can work in an unrestricted manner. The drainage of the soil must be perfect so as to ensure that the land never gets sodden, lime must be given to prevent the soil being too acid, worms must never be eliminated because of the way they help with aeration (see the A.B.C. of Soils, Humus and Health) and

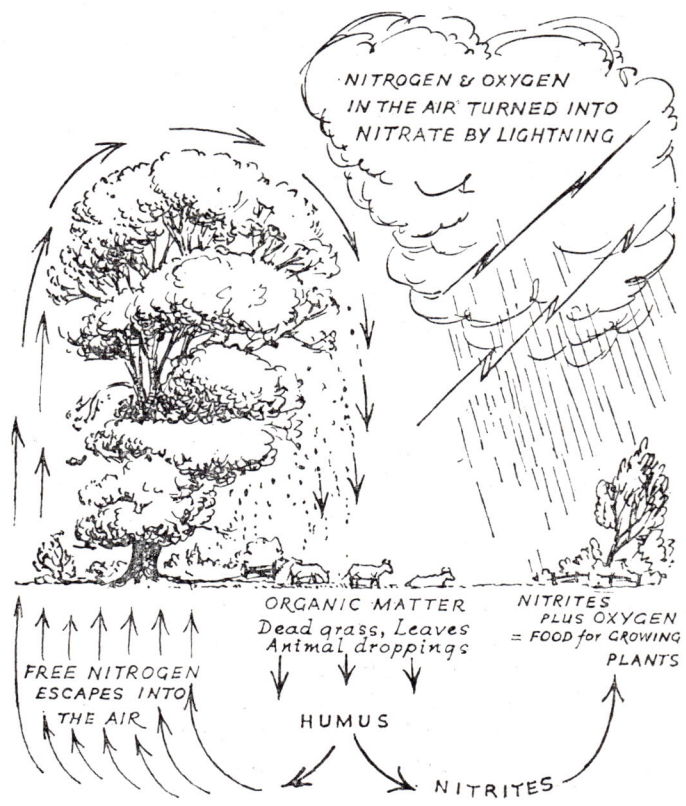

organic matter must be added regularly to provide them with the food they need.

The Cycle or Complete Circle

God's plan from the beginning has been the complete cycle, or circle; the leaves from the trees drop down to the soil in the autumn and are pulled into the ground by the worms – thus organic matter gets back into the soil again. The animals graze the grass in the field and pass back on to the ground the urine and the dung – which in its turn rots down and gets into the soil, forming humus. The dead grass and the dead roots of the grasses get worked on by the earth-worms and even sometimes by the wire-worms and more precious humus is produced. The fly drops to the ground as does the bird, the rabbit dies in its burrow; thus in nature organic matter is constantly passing back into the soil in some way or another.

In addition, owing to lightning a certain amount of nitrogen may be washed into the ground with the rain; further, there are plants like the peas and beans, the clovers and the lupins – all members of the leguminosae family as it is called – that have on their roots bacteria which use the nitrogen and oxygen from the air producing the nitrates. In addition, therefore, to the plant foods produced by humus, there are these two extra sources year by year.

Where is the Manure?

The reader, who by now perhaps is convinced of the importance of adding large quantities of manure each year – is likely to wonder how he is going to get the dung he needs. What is the use of preaching to a beginner when it is almost impossible to buy farmyard manure these days? It is a pity from the gardeners' point of view that the motor-car has taken the place of the horse for the land has suffered grievously as a result, but facts are facts and they must be faced. Fortunately, however, there is an alternative, and it is possible in every garden to make a first-class substitute for farmyard manure with the minimum of time, worry and expense, and without the usual smell associated with dung.

The Compost Heap

Every herb and salad grower should have in his garden, or on his allotment, some corner purposely set aside where all the vegetable waste can be collected for placing in a heap. Some prefer to dig a pit for the purpose, but the disadvantage of the pit is that the rotted material has to be dug out afterwards and this is a tedious job. Further, a pit may easily become sodden with water. To keep the vegetable waste tidy it is convenient to make a three-sided bin, either with old timbers like ex-railway sleepers or with planking treated with Rentokil.

The bin or heap may be of any width and length desired, but for the ordinary garden 4 or 5 foot square should do. It should be allowed to rise to a height of, say, 5 feet, as if it is higher than this it is apt to become unmanageable. As the material in the heap rots down and forms the perfect substitute for dung, the heap reduces in size. (Incidentally, some of the best compost I have produced in my garden has been far more valuable than dung!)

On to the heap and in the bin should be placed all the vegetable waste that can be collected from the house and garden, and even from the hedgerows, fields and trees round about. Those who live in towns can often collect leaves from trees in an avenue or they can obtain plenty of vegetable waste from a local greengrocer's shop. Those who live in the country can collect roadside leaves and grass. In addition, there will always be the waste materials from the house, the tea leaves, the coffee grounds, the peelings from bananas, oranges and the like and where poultry are not kept there will also be the outside leaves of the cabbages, and lettuces as well as the peeling from the various root crops.

From the garden there should be great quantities of organic matter available; the lawn mowings, for instance, the tops of the potatoes and root crops, the haulm (as it is called) of the peas and beans, the tops of the herbaceous plants after they have been cut down, the annuals after they have ceased to flower and the summer clippings from the hedges. One can always use the old cabbage, cauliflower and Brussels sprouts stumps after they have been bashed up well on a chopping block with the back of an axe. There is always something to go on the compost heap, almost every day. The daily newspaper, for instance, if soaked in water, will rot down. There is the fluffy dust that collects in electric and hand sweepers, while those who live by the sea-side can always put on seaweed.

Anything that has lived may therefore go on the compost heap; it is possible to rot down an old mattress, an old woollen or cotton skirt or a pair of woollen trousers, but never Terylene or nylon. It is possible to put on a certain amount of sawdust, though one has to be very careful with this because it takes a long time to rot down when too much is put on at a time. If one keeps rabbits, the droppings go on to the heap, as does, of course, the manure from the poultry.

Into the centre of the heap when it is, say, only a foot or so high, may be driven a post, 3 inches in diameter; the subsequent vegetable waste is then piled around this until it reaches a height of about 4 feet 6 inches, when the post may be carefully pulled out, so as to leave an air vent. This is not absolutely vital but it does help particularly in cases where very soft material is used in large quantities, like lawn mowings.

The Importance of the Activator

For every six-inch thickness of level vegetable waste collected it is advisable and, in fact, necessary to add what is called an activator; this is a product which will encourage and stimulate the micro-organisms and will thus ensure that the vegetable waste, whatever it be, decomposes properly. Actually, decomposes is a bad word for it gives the impression of something going bad. I use it, however, purposely, because to the layman it invariably produces the right picture in his mind. The activator helps to produce an unnatural degree of heating by what can be called natural means; the result is that a bulky, balanced manure is produced free of disease organisms and weed seeds and yet, biologically and minerally rich.

It has been suggested, and there is some empirical proof available, that farmyard manure which is, of course, straw or litter mixed with the dung and urine of animals – is the best activator of all. As, however, it is seldom available, other organic activators may be used instead. It is possible to apply, for instance, dried blood, 'potions' of seaweed and homeopathically applied herbal mixtures. The author has, however, standardised the use of fish manure in his gardens. It is applied as a food to the soil in the greenhouse, as well as in the open and gives first-class results when used on the compost heap as the activator.

Generally speaking one needs about 2 cwt. of fish manure for every one ton of mixed vegetable waste that can be collected.

Those who keep hens may use the poultry manure instead but if it is to be available all the year round, in fact, whenever the next 'layer' of vegetable waste is ready for activation, then after collection it must be stored in a dustbin with a lid. Each bird will give 3 cwt. of droppings a year and it is this weight that is required per one ton of vegetable refuse.

The simple, down-to-earth method is therefore to sprinkle a fish fertiliser at 3 ozs. to the square yard to every level 6-inch thickness of vegetable waste put on the heap and this must be kept level. After the application of the fish manure another 6-inch thickness of refuse may be placed in position – yet another sprinkling of fish manure given and so on. The fish manure, therefore, can be likened to the ham in a ham sandwich. It may take several days to reach the 6-inch thickness or because potatoes are being harvested it may reach a 6-inch thickness in a day or even sooner.

If the soil is acid, or to put it in another way, if the pH is in the region of 5 or 6, then it is necessary to add carbonate of lime to every fourth layer of vegetable waste collected at 6 ozs. to the square yard, instead of the fish manure.* In this case, therefore, three layers are activated with fish while the fourth receives lime. Where soils are on the limey or chalky side, say pH 4 or 3, there is no need to add lime at all and the heat can rise naturally layer by layer using fish manure as an activator *only*.

It does no harm to the compost heap if extra 'helps' are given from time to time; the droppings from pigeons, for instance, or rabbits, or the odd excreta from animals, like goats or dogs. If the bulk of the material appears to be dry then a good deal of water will have to be used to wet it; if possible always place soft material, like lawn mowings, in and among the more fibrous waste like the stems of artichokes or herbaceous plants. Where it is found necessary to put on quantities of cabbage or Brussels sprouts stumps these should be bashed up first with the back of an axe on a chopping block.

Straw takes a good deal of wetting and I have known a

---

* After a few years of using lime on the vegetable garden there is no need to use lime on the compost heap, because the plants will have taken up the Calcium and when put on the compost heap they will pass it back.

1 cwt. bale to mop up 40 gallons of water when stood in an old bath for the purpose of ensuring that it gets sodden. Don't however apply water to such an extent that it flows out from the bottom of the heap.

Turning the Heap

As the drawing shows, it is convenient to have at the side of the bin a dustbin with the lid on holding the fish manure. See that some strong galvanised wire is hooked over the lid from handle to handle, so that it cannot blow away in the first gale. When all this has been done and the heap has been properly made, all one need do when it gets to the height of 5 feet or so is to cover the top with a 3-inch layer of soil which acts as a kind of roof or crust to the loaf, and thus helps to keep the heat in.

Because, however, the outside of the heap will not rot down as well as the inside, keen composters turn their heaps at the end of the first three months with the idea of making the top the bottom and the outsides the inside. During this turning, if any of the material appears to be dry, water may be added. It is seldom necessary, however, at this turning to add any further activator.

THE COMPOST HEAP

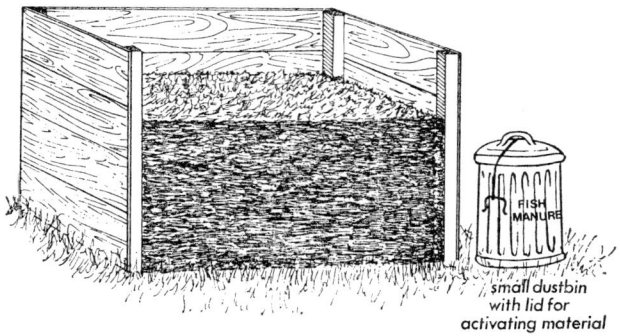

A wooden bin is absolutely necessary to make good compost

The secret of good salads.

Because turning entails so much labour the author seldom, if ever, advises it because, if you insist on turning, readers are just 'put off' composting altogether and at The Good Gardeners' Association gardens at Arkley vast quantities of compost are made every year without any turning at all.

The Organic Fertiliser

In addition to the well-rotted compost which can either be used as a top dressing or mulch, or can be forked or rotovated into the soil, at, say, one heavy barrow load to ten square yards, an organic fertiliser like a fish manure should be applied in addition. The latter is applied as a top dressing over the compost or sedge peat (for the latter is a good substitute for the former) at 3 or 4 ozs. to the square yard. The normal compounded fish fertiliser contains 6 per cent nitrogen, 6 per cent phosphates and sometimes 6 per cent potash.

The fish manure, therefore, is not only used as an activator on the compost heap but, so to speak, as a tonic for plants; sometimes it is applied in the spring at 9 to 4 ozs. to the square yard and for permanent crops like, for instance, many of the herbs, it can be used again with success at a similar rate about the middle of August. Again and again throughout the book instructions are given as to how a fish fertiliser may best be used for each individual crop with which we are dealing.

CHAPTER II

PREPARING, PLANTING AND PROTECTING

HAVING made certain that we have all the organic manure we need to apply we can consider how the soil is to be prepared in order that we may grow our herbs and salads correctly. Incidentally, if there are some of you reading this who have a brand new garden and so you have not been able, as yet, to make compost, may I say, again, that sedge peat is an excellent substitute. (It must be sedge peat and not sphagnum peat.) It may be used at the rate of two bucketfuls to the square yard forked in carefully to the depth of, say, 6 inches. If your soil is sandy and the weather is dry the sedge peat should be soaked first in a bath of water.

One of the simplest ways of preparing the ground is to use a mechanical Rotary Cultivator. This enables the gardener to pulverise the ground (so to speak) in a very short time and to incorporate the compost or sedge peat automatically at the same time. Rotovation does away with digging, but should always be done in the spring and summer and not in the late autumn or winter. If you rotovate soil as late as this it's apt to pan down hard during December, January and February.

Those who have very small gardens, or who cannot afford a petrol driven rotovator, may fork the soil shallowly in the spring. In the late autumn properly prepared powdery compost should be applied all over the land to be used for salad or herb growing, at 1 large barrow load to 4 square yards. It is left there on the surface of the ground until the spring.

Summer Work

Once the ground has been initially prepared by the rotovation or by the spring forking and raking, the main work to be done in the summer is that of hoeing, the idea being to cultivate the soil to the depth of half-an-inch only. In this way the gardener kills the weed seedlings the moment they appear and creates what is called a surface dust mulch. This helps to keep the moisture in the soil below.

Use a Dutch hoe, sharpen both the front and back of the blade, so that when cutting through the soil the hoe works equally well backwards and forwards. This hoe is most effective when the gardener walks backwards slowly, using the hoe in a forwards and backwards movement to cut through the top half-inch of soil and get it into a powdery condition.

It is often advisable to hoe in between the rows of crops; if one can hoe before the weeds appear then there never will be any weeds. Most gardeners find that a draw hoe is only necessary when the weeds have been allowed to grow – and are too long therefore for elimination by the Dutch hoe.

A draw hoe is, however, useful for getting out drills, as is explained later. A draw hoe can also be used for earthing up or for chopping out (as we gardeners put it) the superfluous plants in a row; thus, for instance, those who have sown lettuce seed too thickly in a row can use the draw hoe for 'chopping out' the seedlings and thus leaving little groups of three or four at distances of say, 10 inches apart in the rows. The thinning that has to be done by hand is also necessary to reduce the groups of three or four down to one per station.

Sometimes lumpy land has to be forked over lightly – say, to the depth of 3 inches, with the idea of trying to break it up a little. This forking over can be followed by a methodical treading in order to help break up the lumps. It is possible to buy four- or five-pronged cultivators for stirring the soil. These can be used in between the rows of plants, and especially between the rows of celery before doing any earthing up.

Keen salad growers must produce their crops in the quickest possible time, for it is in this way that one can ensure that they are tender and delicious. A book like this must concentrate on quick production because the great plan is that the crops grown are to be eaten raw. It isn't a question of casting aside old tried practices but it is important to graft on to them ideas which have proved successful under more modern conditions. For instance, we have discovered that the quicker you can get a seed to germinate, the better the result from the salad point of view. Trouble must therefore be taken with the preparation of the seed bed, with watering, and with the addition of an organic substance like fine sedge peat.

Sowing the Seed

Don't attempt to sow any seed until the soil has been properly prepared and until it's in the right physical condition. Seed sowing in sodden soil is fatal. One must wait until it's dried out a little so that the top inch or so of earth can be got into a crumbly condition. It always acts if there is finely divided

Treading a seed-bed with boards strapped to the feet

Getting the soil ready for seed sowing.

organic matter in the top two inches, as well as further well-rotted compost lower down. We gardeners use the words fine tilth – a term not understood by beginners, but it really means that every part of your earth on the surface of the ground where the seed is to be sown is finer than a grain of wheat.

It may be as well to emphasise that one gets this fine tilth as a rule by giving a shallow forking first and then a methodical treading. Some people strap boards onto their boots (as shown in the drawing) because this ensures that the treading is done much more evenly. This treading can be followed by a light raking and then yet another treading perhaps and one more very light raking. This seems a lot of work but for quick germination, a fine tilth is necessary. The raking must be done evenly; that is to say, the head of the rake must be worked backwards and forwards and the larger stones, sticks and other rubbish, removed at the same time. The gardener must aim to get the top ½ inch of soil down really fine, or in the case of the smaller seeds, the top ¼ inch only. No attempt should be made to go any deeper than this.

It may be necessary to wait a few days until the soil is in the right condition. For, as I've already said, you can't prepare an effective seed bed when the ground is wet and sticky – especially in the case of clay land. Sandy soil, of course, can be worked at any time, and those who are lucky enough to have a light soil of this character will be wondering why I am making such a fuss about preparing a fine tilth. On a sandy loam the soil is ready without any special preparation other than the treading or rolling, for sandy soil is apt to be too loose and ' puffy '. Sandy soil, on the other hand, is very hungry and needs much more organic matter added to it than a clay soil.

In the case of heavier soils, the good gardener knows that a dry period followed by a shower often produces the right conditions for preparing a fine tilth. The moisture seems to cause the lumps to crumble and they can be knocked about with the fork, or even if they are trodden they soon break up. There is nothing like experience in a garden, for it is this that teaches a man when the soil is in exactly the right condition for working down fine. Cloches mentioned in detail in Chapter III, are useful for they can be put over a strip of ground that is wet and sticky, and in a few days they will dry it out sufficiently well to ensure the making of a fine seed bed. The author uses them a great deal during the wetter periods for this purpose.

Selecting the Seed

It is very important indeed to go to a good seedsman and pay a fair price for the right variety of salad to be grown. Interestingly enough, there are strains within varieties. Seedsman A, for instance, can have a particularly good strain of variety ' X ', a strain for instance, that is more tender or that is quicker maturing or that has a slightly different colour. One can only learn these facts by trying out the varieties recommended in this book from seedsmen like Unwins in order to discover whether there are particular strains that are better than another. Remember that the cost of the seed itself works out at a very small percentage of the total cost of salad production.

Some have said that it is no more than 5 per cent of the total cost.

Always then, get good seed as well as the right seed for the particular purpose you have in hand, and for the district you have in hand. *It's no good,* for instance, trying to grow an open air variety of lettuce under glass or vice versa. The northerner finds it impossible to grow the specially delicious Roscoff kinds of broccoli which grow so well in Somerset, Devon and Cornwall. Hardier varieties of lettuce are also needed for over-wintering in the northern counties.

The author has made every attempt in the chapters dealing with the various crops to choose the best varieties. But it is not possible in a book of this character to state where they all may be obtained. The varieties required cannot always be obtained from one seedsman; some seedsmen, for instance, seem to specialise in the members of the cabbage family, others, say, in peas and beans, and so on. The keen salad grower may therefore find it necessary to split up his seed order among a few firms for this reason.

Buy the seeds required for the whole season each January, so as to have them ready to hand. Put them in your seed cupboard in tins and use them at the right time. Don't be tempted to rush and try every new novelty that is introduced; this may or may not be good! Sometimes, unfortunately, a so-called novelty *may* be an old variety sent out under a new name. On the other hand, don't be so conservative that you refuse to try anything new because there are times, as for instance, in 1961 when the new dwarf runner bean Hammonds was introduced and proved itself a first-class variety.

SUCCESSFUL SOWING

The actual depth of sowing is determined largely by the size of the seed. The rule of thumb method sometimes advocated, is to multiply the width of the seed by 3 and then to sow it at this depth. A broad bean, therefore, is sown deeper than a pea, and the seed of a parsnip is sown slightly deeper than the seed of parsley. Such a rule is made to emphasise the importance of sowing tiny seeds shallowly. In addition, it is important to bear

PREPARING, PLANTING AND PROTECTING

in mind that seeds may be sown more shallowly in the spring when the ground is moist than in mid-summer when the ground is dry.

Normally, for salad production, seeds are sown in straight evenly spaced lines. This ensures perfect plants with sufficient room for development and makes for ease in subsequent hoeing. A line or cord should be stretched tightly from one end of the plot to the other where the row of seeds is to be sown (the word 'tightly' must be emphasised), and the drill can then be drawn out with the blade of the hoe against the line. The gardener should work backwards keeping his right foot on the line all the time. (Or, of course, his left foot if he is left-handed or, should I say, left-footed!) The little drill must be drawn out to an even depth from one end of the plot to the other and the reason that the line must be kept tight is, of course, that if it is loose the row will not be straight.

Instead of sowing the seed as most people do by sprinkling it thinly along the bottom of the drill thus made, it is better to sow the seed at the actual distances at which the plants are to grow in the rows. This is known as 'station sowing'; for instance, if parsnips are to be eight inches apart then a group of 3 or 4 seeds should be sown at exactly 8-inch distances along the drill and then if all the seed per station should grow it is a simple matter to thin them down to one.

The exception to this rule is in the case of radishes, or of members of the cabbage family, that are to be raised in a seed bed for planting out later. Here the seeds should be sprinkled thinly along the bottom of the drills that have been got out for the purpose.

The 'station sowing' principle may, however, be adopted normally in the case of all seeds with the exception of the peas and beans which, of course, are sown spaced out in the normal way. Further details of methods of sowing will be found in the chapters dealing with the individual crops. However, don't sow, as a rule, in a non-continuous row.

Adopt the station sowing method and this can best be done if the gardener straddles the row, walks forward slowly and takes a pinch of seeds with his thumb and forefinger of the right hand out of the palm of his left hand. Not only will a tremendous amount of seed be saved but a great deal of work avoided afterwards in thinning. Furthermore, the time taken station sowing is no longer than the sowing of a continuous row.

After Sowing

After the seed is sown cover it up, either by raking the ground over lightly or by drawing the soil into the drills with a hoe. I often use the back of the rake for covering the seeds as this seems to move the soil quickly. The next job, and a very important one too, is to compact the soil just above the seeds. This should be done with the back of the rake, holding the handle perpendicular to the soil. It is a kind of pressing motion that is needed. This compacting is specially important in the summer in cases where the soil is likely to be dry afterwards. Expert gardeners on light sandy soil often beat the soil above the seeds with the back of a spade and then rake the surface very lightly afterwards to leave it fine and level. If you do beat the surface of the soil to firm it be sure to hoe lightly with a Dutch hoe in between the rows the moment the seedlings begin to show.

Some seeds germinate very slowly indeed, parsnips are particularly bad in this connection and so is parsley – carrots and onions are not too good. If, therefore, the gardener wishes to be able to see where the lines of the drills are as early as possible, the tip is to include some radish seeds in the particular seed to be sown. The result is that radishes come up very early and mark the rows. They may then be pulled the moment the main vegetable comes through the ground or may be left in the rows until they are fit to use.

In the driest of weather it is sometimes necessary to give the rows a good watering through the fine rose of a watering can – a fine rose is necessary so that the soil is not disturbed when the water is being applied. Such waterings must be thorough and not just mere sprinklings, and for this reasons some gardeners prefer to use the hose with a square area rainer, so that the water may be applied, so to speak, as artificial rain.

Planting

Planting refers to the actual putting out of plants, those as a rule which have been raised in a special seed bed. One should never refer to planting seed. This work is mainly done in connection with members of the cabbage family, the Brussels sprouts, for instance, the kales, cauliflowers and so on. It is, of course, done also in the case of leeks, celery, celeriac. The word planting therefore refers mainly to the setting out of plants which have been raised somewhere else into the positions where they are to crop.

To obtain good plants it is necessary to thin out the seedlings in the seed beds. Seedlings should never be allowed to stand together too thickly otherwise they get long and lanky. Even if the plants are being raised in a frame or under ganwicks they need thinning out. Further, plants raised in greenhouses or in frames must be properly hardened off before they are planted in the open. This means that ten days or so before they are to be planted, more and more ventilation must be given until they are quite used to outside conditions. Thus they get the minimum of check.

It is wise to soak the seed bed thoroughly with water before removing the plants so that when they are carefully forked out they have a good ball of moist soil at their roots. If a thorough soaking is given, say, the day before, the leaves of the plants will be really firm and turgid. The plants being charged with water will be able the more easily to stand up to windy or droughty conditions or both.

It is always better to plant or transplant in dull, cloudy or showery weather. If, however, the work has to be done when the weather is hot and dry, a good tip is to make a mixture of clay and water to the consistency of cream in a bucket and then to swish the roots well in this before putting them in the ground. Where there is time the holes made with the trowel or dibber may be filled with water at planting time – this being allowed to drain away a little before the plant is put in. Plants lifted from a seed bed for transplanting must not be out of the ground longer than is absolutely necessary. If they have to be out for some time, keep them covered with a wet sack. Some gardeners take the trouble in very droughty weather to do the transplanting at night time for then they have a number of hours of darkness in which to recover!

If the leaves of the plants are very large and the weather is

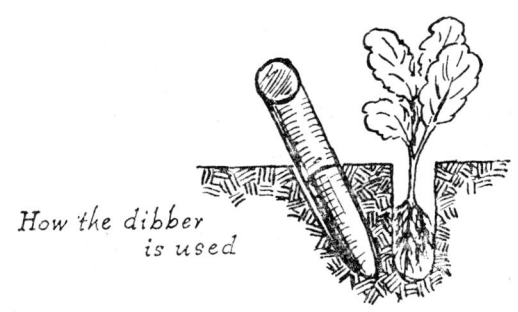

How the dibber is used

Shortening leaves by a half when transplanting

Planting with a trowel
Note that firming is done with the handle

Planting.

very dry it's possible to cut the foliage in half – as shown in the drawing on page 30. Leaf evaporation is thus reduced by 50 per cent. I always shorten the leaves of leeks by half when planting whether it is dry or no.

Using a Dibber or Trowel

In practice it is always better to use a trowel rather than a dibber for a bigger hole is made and the plant roots have thus a better chance of spreading out properly. Further, with a dibber, there is always the danger of leaving an air-pocket just below the bottom of the root and/or having smooth, over-compacted soil. Planting with a dibber on the whole is quicker and one can make certain that there are no air pockets, if the dibber is used sideways on at planting to firm the base of the roots rather than the soil around the upper part of the stems. (Please see drawing on page 30.)

The best way of using a dibber is to push it in downwards, giving it half a turn as you do so, so that it enters more easily. Then lower the plant into the hole seeing that the root is not bent upwards at the base and so that the roots are completely buried up to the bottom seed leaves of the plant. In cases where the main tap root is extremely long it is sometimes necessary to reduce it by about a quarter by cutting off the bottom with a sharp knife or a pair of scissors. The dibber should then be inserted at an angle of 45 degrees or so, one inch away from the plant with the idea of pressing the soil firmly against the roots. The dibber is then levered up towards the plant as shown in the drawing.

Planting should be done so tightly that if the gardener catches hold of the tops of the leaves of the plant, these will pull off before the plant will draw out of the soil. It is the roots which must be fixed tightly into the soil, that is why the earth must be firmed below ground level and not actually at ground level as so many people do.

When planting with the trowel a good hole can be made and this is especially useful if there is a ball of soil to the roots. The plant should be held in the centre of the hole with one hand and the other hand used to firm the soil around the root. I always take the trowel by its blade and then use the handle to press the soil down and around the roots and thus I can make it really compact. Water can always be poured into the hole just prior to planting but should not be poured into the hole after the soil is put back prior to firming because it is then too much of a mud puddle for correct firming to be possible.

By the way, the side hole that you make in the case of dibber planting need not be filled up and this can always be filled with water a few hours after planting if necessary.

Watering

As most vegetables contain about 80 per cent water and some well over 30 per cent, it may be necessary in dry seasons to give 'artificial rain' so as to ensure the production of succulent vegetables and salads needed by those who are going to eat them raw. If these are grown without sufficient moisture they can be low in sugar content and may therefore be slightly bitter. Remember the advice given in Chapter I with regard to the rotting down of vegetable waste and the addition of finely divided organic matter to the soil. Where the humus content of the soil is high there is far less a problem with regard to soil moisture than when the earth is very low in humus.

The advantage of overhead watering is that it enables the gardener to have his vegetables and salads in a succulent condition even during a continuous drought. When plants are able to grow without a check they are never as badly attacked by pests as when they have a check owing to drought. Watering helps to stimulate the soil bacteria. May I emphasise, however, that it is fatal to try and make up for bad feeding by watering – you should never water impoverished land. Further, the water should always be applied through a fine hose for it should be in a condition similar to rain.

It is always better to water before forking or digging because most soils absorb water more easily when in a fairly solid condition than when loose. This is especially so if the surface of the soil is loose, for then it soon becomes sodden and the water will not penetrate below. Having then watered a strip of ground, dig it or fork it over an hour or so afterwards, leave longer if heavy soil. One can always water after seeds are sown and at any time during the summer in droughty periods. Excellent

PREPARING, PLANTING AND PROTECTING

results are achieved if the watering is done when the temperature of the soil is high. I use a sprinkler which covers a square area and which produces artificial rain in a fine state. In very dry weather it is necessary to apply water once or twice a week at the rate of 25 gallons per hour per quarter of an acre.

As a general rule the overhead sprinkler will have to be left in a particular position for at least three-quarters of an hour, for if the water is to be given it must be applied at a heavy rate.

The very light sprinkling of water with the watering can, so often done by the beginner, is not only wasteful of time and water, but may do harm. If it is impossible to water thoroughly, it is better not to water at all but to rely more and more on there being plenty of organic matter in the ground, plus sedge peat as a mulch on top of the ground.

Protection

It is sometimes necessary to give protection to plants. Chapter III which follows, for instance, gives details of the protection which may be provided by cloches or Access Frames, while Chapter IV shows how English or Dutch frame lights may be used instead. I have seen gardeners give protection by using calico or sacking 'shields' which can be laid over a skeleton frame of wood built temporarily tent-wise over a crop. Pea-sticks or brushwood are sometimes placed loosely over plants in the winter to give some protection from frost. Little 'fences' a foot or so high may be made on either side of a bed or a row of plants for the purpose of keeping off the cold winds in the winter.

Plants set out in shallow furrows for protection

Planting out cabbage seedlings.

These temporary fences may be made of pea-sticks or strips of sacking of the right height.

Plants need protection from the soil surface cold winds in the winter and from the bright sunshine in the hottest weather in the summer. In the latter case screens of lattice-work or sacking may be erected to provide shade. Some protection can be given in the early spring if the plants are set out in shallow furrows or drills instead of on the flat. (See drawing page 33.)

CHAPTER III

THE USE OF CLOCHES

ONE of the difficulties of getting people to use cloches is that you can't believe how valuable they are and what a difference they make, until you have had them in use for a month or two. Once a cloche user – always a cloche user, especially in the case of those who wish to grow tender fresh food to use without cooking. It isn't any use, however, just buying one or two cloches, because these do not give the desired effect. It is only when several cloches are linked together that the area of warmth becomes sufficient to hasten the growth of the plants.

Cloches give all the protection needed to plants growing outside during the winter. They therefore enable salads to be picked in winter when in the normal way they are either very expensive to buy or impossible to get at all. If the cloches are put into position over a strip of land a fortnight before sowing, they warm the ground and the surface can be got down to a fine tilth. Sowings can thus be made outside on quite sticky land in a cold month like January or February.

Cloches give the plants protection from mud splashes due to rain, and thus salads are particularly palatable and do not have to be washed thoroughly as they do in the normal way. Cloches give almost perfect germination owing to the warmth and seeds are thus saved. Under cloches crops mature more quickly and because they are not so long on the ground, more crops can be got per year from any area of land available.

Where only a small quantity of each thing is needed it is quite possible to grow two crops under one cloche, or even three, providing care is taken that they do not shade one another or make hoeing difficult. For instance, a row or two of lettuce can be planted to the sunny side of a row of peas or broad beans, or else a row of double cloches can be made to shelter both 4 rows of carrots and 2 rows of lettuce, the lettuce being planted under one half, the carrots under the other.

This is really better than the old practice of alternating each row of lettuce with a row of carrots, for this tends to 'draw' the leaves of the carrots which get too much shade from the lettuce – and it is a pity, for it is those with stocky, deep green tops that mature most quickly. The lettuces too, are healthier when only grown in proximity to their own kind, as they require plenty of air and a soil that is kept free from weeds if they are to heart quickly and show no signs of botrytis.

Cloches are self ventilating, while at the same time affording complete protection. When hoeing or hand-weeding becomes necessary, the removal of a top or side pane (or both if preferred) will give complete and easy access to the crop. If the first pane (or panes) removed are clipped at once to the end of the row, all subsequent ones can be shunted back one space as one works along the row, thus avoiding having to handle the glass twice.

There are three methods of watering plants growing under flat-topped-cloches; (a) by overhead application, (b) by hand-directed jet, (c) by trickle irrigation.

Method (a): Cloches are made in such a way that any water falling on them will be automatically directed inside; thus, spraying the top of the glass with an oscillating spray or otherwise will effectively water the crop, but it is as well to remember that this overhead application of cold water will considerably lower the temperature of the cloches – which can be troublesome in cold, dull weather.

Method (b): For larger plants, such as marrows, tomatoes, etc., it is possible to direct the jet of a hose-pipe through the ventilation gaps between the sides or top panes.

Method (c): Trickle lines which are laid *inside* the cloches or access frames (one line down the centre of each span is sufficient) is undoubtedly the most trouble-free method of watering and also the best, for the water applied in this way has time to get warm as it flows slowly through the small pipes, and thus never lowers the temperature inside the cloches or access frames. It also has the added advantage of not wetting the leaves of the plants and not wasting water unnecessarily on the pathways.

It is possible to grow some crops under cloches from start to finish, a typical example being the lettuce. Often, however, cloches are used to cover rows of crops to bring them on earlier, and then, when they are three-quarters grown or when they are touching the tops of the cloches, these are removed and used for other crops. The same cloches can be used to cover successive sowings of peas, or any other vegetable or salad. Cloches give protection from birds, protection from east winds and wetness. They are easily moved about, they are rigid and not easily broken, and are not liable to be blown over in strong winds or even gales.

Soil Preparation

It is necessary to prepare the soil for cloches as advised in Chapter I. It will be necessary to fork the surface over to get the soil down as fine as possible, and to break up the clods by treading, followed by a raking to get the soil level and the particles into a sufficiently fine condition. At the same time the compost or sedge peat will be added.

As the importance of the use of organic matter was stressed in Chapter I there is no need to deal with it in further detail here, except to say that it is almost more important to have plenty of finely divided organic matter in the top 3 inches of soil under cloches than in the open. This helps to hold the moisture and produces a better mechanical and physical condition. Sedge peat (often damped first) should be forked in to the top inch or two of soil at a bucketful to the square yard. Any fertilisers used should be those with an organic base, such as a fish manure at 5-6 oz. to the square yard.

Soot is useful under cloches for it helps to darken light soils, and enables them thus to retain the heat better. As it is a nitrogenous manure it should also be used mainly in the case of the cabbage family. If potash is needed, which it often is, especially where soils are light, wood ashes may be used at 4-5 oz. per square yard during the preparation of the soil.

Lastly, lime should be given as a top dressing, especially in the case of acid soils. It adds calcium as a plant food, and because it helps to decompose humus and organic compounds it ensures that other plant foods are released. It sweetens the soil, improves its texture, making those that are sticky, more workable.

B*

It should be applied to the surface of the ground after the other manures have been dug or forked in. Hydrated lime is ideal to use at the rate of 3, 4 or 5 oz. to the square yard, according to the acidity of the soil.

Seed Sowing
The advice given in Chapter II on sowing seeds should certainly be followed under cloches, for germination under these miniature greenhouses is perfect.

Sun
Arrange the rows running east and west and thus obtain the minimum amount of shade in the winter months. Cloches cannot manufacture sunshine, they can only trap it. So always try to have the cloches in a sunny position.

Early and Late Crops
Cloches enable seeds to be sown in June and July in the open, then in the autumn the resultant crops can be covered to give the winter supplies. Again, sowing may be done in November and January for early spring.

Endives
It is not always realised how useful cloches can be for blanching Endives. The various methods of blanching usually practised all tend to hamper the normal life of the plant and make it more susceptible to rot, as in the case when they are either lifted bodily and packed in cold frames, or else tied up in the manner of cos lettuce, and straw or litter packed round them. With cloches it is possible to allow them to remain in the bed in which they have been raised, and place the cloches over them. If extra panes of glass are available, two panes should be inserted each time instead of one, with a thick sheet of brown paper slipped between them. The wire frames hold the glass sufficiently loosely for this to be quite easy, and the paper will not only effectively blanch the endives, but further prevent loss of heat through the glass.

Endives are best sown in their final positions, successional sowings being made from June to September. Four rows can be accommodated under double cloches, and the plants should be thinned to 9 inches apart.

Mustard and Cress

Mustard and cress is easily grown under cloches at all times of the year, except mid-winter. The soil should be rich in humus and worked to a very fine tilth. Seed is best sown broadcast (the cress should be sown three days before the mustard as it takes that much longer to germinate) and pressed lightly into the soil with a wooden seed-press, then well watered in. To ensure rapid and even growth, the soil should never be allowed to get really dry, and the best method of watering is with a fine rose, having first removed the top panes of the cloches. When ready, mustard and cress should always be cut with scissors.

Corn Salad

Corn salad or Lambs Lettuce (known in France as ' màché ') is a useful salad for the autumn and winter months if given glass protection. It is the rounded leaves of this plant that are picked, in the same manner as spinach. Successional sowings should be made from June to September, four rows to a double cloche, and the plants thinned out to about 8 inches apart. This crop should be hoed frequently, as it hates weeds, and the cloches should be put in position in October.

Parsley

Parsley is really a perennial and can be kept alive for several years if given the protection of cloches from November to April. Before covering the row should be hoed and cleaned up, all the old, coarse leaves being removed so as to stimulate young growth.

When treating parsley as an annual, the two main times for sowing are March and August. The seeds are very slow to germinate, but the March sowing can be hastened by a covering with cloches, which should have been in position a good fortnight to warm the soil. The seedlings are better thinned to 6 inches apart. The August sowing can be done in the open, and is especially valuable for producing a good crop of fresh young leaves in the early spring when given winter protection.

Silver-Skin Onions

There is another salad crop which is rarely thought of : silver-skin onions. In seed catalogues they are only listed for pickling, but, if sown under cloches in February, they make excellent salad onions at a time when the September-sown 'spring onions' are getting rather too large. The soil should be well warmed up before sowing, and the onions sown thinly in drills 4 to 6 inches apart. Paris Silver Skin is the most suitable variety for this purpose.

Beet

Round or salad beet can be had very early when grown under cloches*, which should be placed in position well in advance to warm the soil before actually sowing. A double cloche will take five rows of beet, and, for the plant to grow quickly, they should be thinned as soon as possible. It is no use hoping that sowing thinly will obviate the irksome task of thinning, for beetroot 'seeds' are really an agglomeration of seeds, which will each produce a little cluster of seedlings. How early it is wise to sow depends very much on the locality, the season, and the type of soil, but it will be safe to say that globe beet should be among the first sowings of the year.

* In every case where cloches are mentioned – there is always the opportunity of using Access Frames. These are similar to square Ganwicks except that they are linked together.

CHAPTER IV

THE USE OF DUTCH LIGHTS AND FRAMES

MUCH use can be made of frames both heated and cold for the growing of vegetable and salad crops throughout the autumn, winter and early spring, when there is obviously a scarcity outside. The heated frame of course gives the ideal conditions and especially so as this heat can be thermostatically controlled. It is in this way that the temperature of the soil can be kept at some definite level. It is not too expensive to heat the soil in frames electrically and your local Electricity Board will be glad to supply you with a free booklet on the subject called ' Electricity in the Garden ', and give you advice.

Garden owners who have installed modern forms of central heating in the home have sometimes found it possible to use the hot water for frames which are purposely erected close to the house. They arrange, for instance, that 2-inch pipes run right round the frames to provide the necessary heat.

Firms that are responsible today for installing oil burners and gas burners for household hot water heating will also be able to advise on the use of 2-inch piping in a frame or even in a greenhouse or conservatory which could be built on to the side of a house.

When it is not advisable or possible to heat a frame electrically or by means of hot water pipes – the alternative is to make up what is called a ' hot bed '. Basically the need here is for horse manure which is put into the bottom of the frame to the depth of at least a foot and preferably 18 inches. Over the top of this is placed the soil in which the plants are to be grown, to the depth of about 6 inches. The decomposing horse manure produces heat which warms the soil above and the crops benefit in consequence. Furthermore, of course, at the end of the winter season when the manure is dug out, it can be used as organic matter for the salad plot outside.

There is of course today a great shortage of horse manure and because of this some gardeners have used as a substitute rotting vegetable waste. This does not give as much heat as decomposing dung nor does it go on producing the heat for as long a time. However, it is better to use some type of hot bed and alternatives are cow manure or pig manure mixed with vegetable waste or poultry manure as a kind of sandwich in layers of straw. The reason however that people have adopted soil heating by means of electrically heated wires is that it is simple, clean, effective and (if the instructions are carried out) not dangerous.

To get the best results with any method of soil heating the compost or soil mixture used above such a hot bed should be as full of finely divided organic matter as possible. The French always mix the last year's hot bed with the last year's frame surface soil. They call this substance 'terreau'. This black, spongy, well rotted organic matter full of humus gives rise to ideal plants. Sometimes it is possible to buy old mushroom bed material from a mushroom farm; this, too, is an excellent medium in the frame if mixed with half its bulk of good soil.

A frame which is to be covered with three frame lights 6 feet 6 inches long and 4 feet 6 inches wide needs 1 ton of horse manure compacted tightly underneath the soil to produce the necessary heat required to grow, say, lettuce plants throughout the winter. This horse manure will be trodden down to a depth of 9 inches and will then be covered with the terreau to a depth of about 6 inches. As it is usually desired to have a slight slope to the top of the frame so as to allow the rain to run off, it may be necessary to put the terreau on to the hot bed 6 inches deep at the back and only 4 inches deep at the front. This special compost should then be made firm by pressing it down with flat wooden presses. The bed should be made about the middle of January as a rule, with the result that if the planting is done correctly the lettuces will be ready to cut in March or April.

Those who are taking the trouble to make up a hot bed, or who are going to the expense of putting in electrical soil heating, will want to get the most out of their frames and this can be done best by growing three or four crops at a time. In January the seed of a special carrot called 'Demi Longue-à-Forcer' should be broadcast all over the surface of the terreau and be lightly raked in, the aim being to do the sowing a week after the hot bed has been made up, or the electricity turned on. This should be followed immediately by the planting out of seedlings of lettuce 1 inch high of the variety Gotte-â-Forcer. The plants of this lettuce must be raised by sowing the seeds fairly thickly under cloches or in a cold frame at the beginning of the second week of October, the seedlings that result being planted out when they are $\frac{1}{2}$-inch high, 2 inches apart under cloches.

We now have two crops in the frame and about the beginning of April the seeds of our next crop must be sown. This is a special variety of turnip called like the carrot, Demi Longue-à-Forcer, and 9 seeds should be sown at stations 10 inches apart in between the rows of lettuce which have been planted 10 inches square also. We now have 3 crops in the frame. Five days later, cauliflower plants are set out one at each corner of the frame and one in the middle, i.e. 5 plants go into each frame.

These cauliflower plants have been raised by sowing the seed at the end of August in a sunny bed in the open where sedge peat has been forked in at a bucketful to the square yard. The young plants thus raised are planted out under cloches or in cold frames, 3 inches square, early in October. They are therefore 5 or 6 inches high by the time they are planted in April. The variety in this case is all the year round.

All this time the frames are not ventilated at all. The glass lights, in fact are kept tightly in position. The moment, however, the lettuces are cut in April plenty of air may be given and, in fact, when all the lettuces have been used the glass lights may be removed altogether and the frames given a thorough flooding with water. From this time onwards watering can be done every third or fourth day and good ventilation ensured by raising the top and bottom of the lights alternately by means, say, of an ordinary brick.

The turnips will be pulled the moment they are sufficiently large sized to be used and the carrots will be harvested soon afterwards. You can then, if you wish, move the frame lights to another part of the garden to grow, say, melons and so leave the cauliflowers growing in their original spot until they are cut early in June.

One can always help to conserve heat in the frames by surrounding them with plenty of straw. This can be put on as high as the lights and will keep out draughts. In the winter, during very frosty periods, the tops of the frames may be covered with sacking, or it is possible to make special 'eiderdowns' with plenty of dry straw put into old sacks the size of the frame lights. These are then just laid on top.

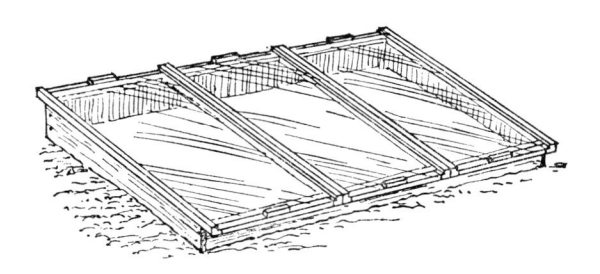

Dutch light frames

Growing with Dutch Lights

Up till now the method described in detail has been what the gardener calls 'French Gardening'. We now come to the use of Dutch lights, a system which has come to us from Holland. The Dutch light consists of a single pane of horticultural glass, measuring 56 inches by $28\frac{3}{4}$ inches; this is held in a wooden frame consisting of top and bottom rails, $2\frac{1}{2}$ inches by $1\frac{1}{2}$ inches and sides styles, 2 inches by 2 inches. Grooves are provided in the styles or rails and the big sheet of glass is slipped into these. A wooden stop, is provided in the bottom rails so as to prevent the frame slipping down further. When made up the whole Dutch light is 59 inches long and $31\frac{3}{4}$ inches wide.

Sometimes Common Deal is used, treated with a preservative such as Rentokil, and on other occasions the wood is Western

Red Cedar which is more lasting and need not be treated. The disadvantage of using Dutch lights is that when breakage occurs there is a whole expensive pane to replace; on the other hand, this light throws much less shade than the normal English or French frame light which consists, say, of twenty panes of glass plus two wooden bars on which the squares of glass rest.

Choose a situation for the frame, or frames, where there is plenty of sunshine – preferably land with a very slight fall to the south. With Dutch lights it is usual to use ordinary soil and to grow the crops cold. The lights protect the plants from excessive rain and wind and ensure that the soil temperature is higher and the atmosphere warmer than in the case of crops growing in the open. This does not mean to say that you cannot use Dutch lights with soil heating and, once again, it is a very good thing to consult the senior official of the local Electricity Board who should have all the information available on the subject.

Very often the frames used are quite temporary in character, they may consist of planks of wood, 9 inches wide and 1 inch thick at the back and $4\frac{1}{2}$ inches wide and 2 inches thick in the front. The wood may be Rentokil-treated Deal, or better still, Western Red Cedar. The top surface of the boards should be planed in such a manner that when the Dutch lights lie on them there is a perfect fit. The front and back boards should be kept upright by being nailed to stakes of Deal or Cedar, 2 inches wide and 2 inches thick and 3 feet long. These are driven into the ground at equal distances so that the boards may be nailed to them. Some will be needed at the front of the frame and the others at the back.

For covering up the lights during frosty periods, it is possible to buy special Dutch mats made up of reeds, 10 feet long and 5 feet 6 inches wide; these should be stored in a dry place when not in use. Gardeners who are full of ingenuity can fix up a little spray line in the frame so that the watering can be done automatically. By the way, arrange the frames to run East and West so that the plants will get the maximum sun in the winter.

Cropping the Frames

There are a number of varieties of lettuce like May King, May Queen and Attractie which are ideal for growing under Dutch lights in frames during the winter and early spring when the light conditions are poor. A start should be made by sowing the seed in boxes containing the No-Soil compost. The seedlings, as soon as they are $\frac{1}{2}$ an inch high, should be planted 2 inches apart each way into other boxes containing the same compost. A first sowing can be made in October and further sowings, if necessary, every fortnight for two months or so, with the idea of ensuring a succession of plants.

The frames should be on a slightly raised bed and the soil should be well prepared by raking and forking and so be of a good tilth. It should be 6 inches from the light at the back of the frame, and 4 inches from the light at the front of the frame, and should be made moderately firm with a flat wooden presser. It is into such soil that the seedlings will be pricked out 2 inches by 2 inches. The plants should not be watered overhead afterwards, nor should the rain be allowed to fall on them. Keep the lights closed for a few days till the seedlings are established and then ventilate gradually.

The seedlings from such frames will be planted out into further properly prepared frames some time in January, the site chosen being slightly sheltered and having a gentle slope to the south or south-east. It is usual to prepare such a frame in November to give the soil time to settle, and ordinary farmyard manure or well-rotted vegetable refuse will be dug in then at one good barrowload to 8 square yards. Into the top 3 or 4 inches of soil will be forked sedge peat at $\frac{1}{2}$ lb. to the square yard and fish manure with a 6 per cent potash content at 3 ounces to the square yard.

The soil will then be raked thoroughly so that the level is about 6 inches from the top of the back of the frame and 4 inches from the top of the front of the frame. The lights are then put into position so that the soil has a chance of warming up 14 days before planting. It is as well to cover them with mats to protect from excessive frost and wet. The sides of the frame should be banked up well with soil to exclude draughts, and if plenty of straw is put on the pathway in front of the frame, it prevents the soil from puddling and ensures good drainage below.

Before the lettuce is planted, carrots should be sown in rows dropping the seeds ½ inch apart and then raking over lightly afterwards. Good varieties are Amsterdam Forcing, Early Gem, or Sweetheart. Hydrated lime should then be applied as a top dressing at the rate of 3 ounces to the square yard and the soil lightly firmed with a wooden presser, made about 2 feet by 1 foot. The lettuce plants raised in the other frames should be then planted 10 inches square, care being taken that the roots system remain intact. Each seedling should sit on the soil. It should not be buried too deeply. Firm planting is essential.

After the lettuces are in, the frame lights should be put on and should be kept closed, no ventilation being given except after a bad frost at night time, when ventilation may be given at the bottom to ensure that the thaw is gradual and takes place before the sun strikes on the plants. When the frost is out of the frame, close the lights again. Some ventilation may be given when the plants are getting larger, say, in April, for 1 hour during the hottest part of the day. The lettuces will be cut before the carrots are pulled as a rule.

Other Methods

Radishes may be sown in frames any time from January to March and grow very satisfactorily. Carrots may be sown alone early in September and October to provide good roots in the late spring. Spinach may be sown in February or early March and as a result is usually fit to use early in April. Mustard and cress, of course, is a crop that can be grown in frames at almost any time of the year. As the mustard germinates more rapidly than the cress it should be sown 3 days after the latter and it is quite a good plan to sow the seed on damp sacking laid on the soil to prevent the seedlings from carrying up the grit during their growth. ½ lb. of mustard seed, or 6 ounces of cress seed are needed for every 1 square yard. Don't cover the seed with soil after sowing, but put sacking over the top, for the seed seems to germinate best in darkness.

Beetroot

May be grown in frames but doesn't like being forced. Sow from mid-January onwards, in rows 10 inches apart. Thin out to 4 inches apart, but see Chapter II about 'station' sowing. Ventilate on warm days when they are growing well and take the lights off altogether on the warmest dry days when the plants grow taller.

Spinach

Spinach, when grown in these frames is very delicious for salads – the seed is usually broadcast thinly over the surface of the soil during the first week in March and a light raking is given afterwards. As a result the first true leaves should appear in about 4 weeks and the Dutch lights can then be removed if they are needed for other purposes. The spinach should be ready to cut before the end of April. Some people have sown seed in February for cutting in March.

Carrots

In order to ensure a supply of fresh young carrots in the winter, seed of a frame variety may be sown broadcast in September or early October and the small plants given a protection by the frames during the winter. The carrots will be pulled in the spring as and when necessary.

Cucumbers

It is possible, of course, to raise frame cucumbers under Dutch lights provided fermenting manure is dug in below so that bottom heat can be supplied. The aim is to try and stabilise the temperature in the frames at about 80 degrees F. In the early stages put mats or old sacks over the Dutch lights, but directly the seedlings appear these covers are removed, only being replaced at night time. The seed should be sown about a month before the plants are needed for putting out into other frames.

The planting of the crop usually occurs during the second week of April – one plant being put under each Dutch light over the hotbeds which have been prepared with the manure. The frames are then kept closed for three days and after this a certain amount of ventilation can be given. It is usual to shade the Dutch lights by squirting some lime water over the glass in July. After this the treatment is similar to the advice given in Chapter XIII.

CHAPTER V

THE GROWING OF HERBS

THERE is no doubt that as a country we are becoming more and more herb minded. More and more people are taking continental holidays than ever before with the result that they are experimenting in the kitchen with lots of 'foreign dishes'. It is here that herbs come into their own and it has been said that one can only cook superbly when herbs are used intelligently. Herbs, in fact, bring the fragrance of the spring and summer right the way throughout the year in cooking.

To have them at their best they must be grown well in soil rich in humus, the harvesting has to be done at the right time, the drying carried out correctly and intelligently (more of this later on), and then the storing has to be done in glass jars with air-resistant stoppers. These, if the colour of the herbs is to be retained, should be wrapped around with blue paper.

It is difficult to draw the line of demarcation between the culinary herbs and the medicinal ones, for there are plants which are coveted by the cooks for their flavours and yet are considered just as important medicinally. Some people have tried to show a difference by classing the culinary herbs as 'sweet' herbs but this is equally misleading, because there are plants like Southernwood which are bitter and certainly not sweet. Nearly all herbs today are cultivated and this especially applies to those used in cooking. The herbalists may go out into the countryside seeking special herbs for their cures but we gardeners grow those that we need in a border, preferably near the kitchen.

During the last few years the author has made a great feature of the narrow kitchen herb border; he was able to demonstrate it one afternoon on I.T.V. showing how the busy housewife can do her best with her herbs if she is able to go out of her kitchen door and collect what she needs in two or three minutes. The herb border therefore need not be wider than 2 or 3 feet and can be as long as will take all the herbs that are to be grown planted, say, in rows 18 inches apart. Each herb row should be clearly labelled and in order to keep down weeds the soil should be covered with sedge peat to a depth of one inch. This is a perfect mulch that will make hoeing unnecessary and furthermore, the organic matter will be revelled in by the herbs themselves.

Though it is extremely useful to be able to dry and store herbs for the winter time, there is no doubt that you get the best piquancy from them when you eat them in their fresh state. Powdered fresh herbs give a wonderful flavour to stews and soups, fresh herbs chopped up fine make all the difference in the world to the salad bowl, while there are some herbs which add a flavour and coolness to a cider or claret cup.

There are some housewives who never go farther than using mint, parsley, sage and thyme. The object of this chapter, however, is to try and persuade all readers to grow a much larger selection of herbs even if a number of them are mixed together afterwards, to produce the 'mixed herbs' which are so useful. When growing herbs it is important to see that none of them spread beyond the confines allotted to them. Mint can be a great offender but fortunately it is an extremely simple herb to grow and the more you cut it about and injure it the more it seems to survive and the better crop it produces.

One word of warning before we start even to think about growing the different kinds of herbs that are available and that is, beware of heavy-handedness. There is always a danger that because you are growing your own herbs and have therefore plenty of them that you use them in a big way. It is when the soupçon of a herb is used that you get the wonderful flavour which makes everybody say what a good cook you are. But when you use too much, the dish will promptly be nondescript and you will have lost that light, delicate touch that marks the French Chef.

Let us now take the various herbs one at a time and give details as to their cultivation and use. Remember that it is possible to raise the great majority of them by seed sowing and those who have difficulty in getting the necessary seeds may write to me enclosing a stamped, addressed envelope.

ALECOST (*Tanecutum balsamita*)

This old-fashioned herb is often known as Costmary – it bears daisy-like flowers, yellow in colour on stems about 3 feet tall. Plant it in a warm sunny place and it will flower in August, but to keep it going, it is best to divide the plants and re-plant in the October or early November of each year.

It is not difficult to propagate by the division of roots and this can be done either in October, as has already been said, or in the spring. Be sure, however, to plant firmly, a foot apart in the rows. It is not fussy about soil and I have had it growing happily in a heavy clay and in a gravelly sand.

The leaves should be picked up in the summer whenever they are needed for adding to a salad. They impart a very pleasant minty flavour; some people like them as a flavouring for sandwiches for this reason. Incidentally, we use the foliage when bruised to rub into bee and wasp stings and it proves to be very soothing indeed.

ANISE (*Pimpinella anisum*)

This is a dainty annual plant which only grows 12 inches high. It has a very strong flavour and this is the reason why many people do not use it.

If, however, a few leaves are cut up and put in a salad they do add a piquant flavour. Leaves should never be put in whole but should be cut up well first.

Choose a warm sunny situation. Sow the seed thinly and shallowly in April in rows 1 foot apart, also, if necessary, transplant the thinnings one foot square. It is necessary to water carefully after transplanting, for anise does not like being moved.

It is possible to raise plants by sowing seeds in boxes filled with 'No-Soil' Seed Compost in March and then transplanting the seedlings out into the open about mid-May. The transplanting should be done with a good ball of soil on the roots. If you like the flavour of aniseed you should certainly grow this herb and use it. The French love it as a drink!

BALM (*Melissa offcinalis*)

Here is one of the favourite Mediterranean herbs much beloved by bees; in fact, it is said if you have plenty of Balm in the garden the bees will never leave their hive for another! It is a mild, sweet smelling herb with rather small white flowers. The leaves have a lemon flavour and scent and it is a herb that is perhaps used in larger quantities than any other.

It is certainly not particular as to soil and situation; it will grow almost anywhere but it always does best in soil that has been enriched with lots of old compost or sedge peat. It can easily be propagated by the division of roots in the autumn or by the sowing of seed in May. It produces a plant usually 18 inches high with square, erect stems.

In the case of seed sowing, drills should be got out 12 inches apart and ½ inch deep and the seeds must be sown thinly in these. When the seedlings are through the ground they are thinned out to 6 inches apart and finally to 18 inches apart. Each autumn or winter the plants should be cut down almost to ground level and they will grow up again strongly the following spring.

Fruit juices and fruit cups are improved by adding one or two leaves of Balm. Fruit salads are more delicious when some finely chopped Balm leaves are added sparsely, the same applies to raw salads and soups. Dried leaves are added to a stuffing 'mixture' for poultry. A special 'tea' is made by boiling the leaves and this is said to be a good remedy for colds. Many country folk add 1 part of dried Balm leaves to 2 parts of tea and thus they produce, they say, a more refreshing liquid.

BASIL
Bush Basil   (*Ocymum minimum*)
Sweet Basil   (*Ocymum basilicum*)

The Basils are said to be the most strongly flavoured aromatic herbs grown in Great Britain. The flavour of these two Basils is certainly very similar and in most years my wife is able to make two good harvests for dried leaves. We found in Italy that Basil was known as the tomato herb because it is used almost entirely with tomato dishes. It is a herb, by the way, that gives up its flavour only when cooked and because it is so strong it must be used very sparingly.

I have been asked sometimes to describe the flavour of Basil and I have said that it is a mixture of cloves, orange peel and mint, and that is as near as I can get to describing it! We grow Basil as an annual because in cold wet winters it doesn't keep growing out-of-doors.

Sow the seed in March in rows 18 inches apart and thin the plants out to 9 inches apart in the rows. Those who live in the North may need to use square glass cloches* for the purpose, and then having got the plants going these can be removed in June. If the cloches are put back again during the third week of September the Basil can be kept going throughout the winter.

The alternative is to sow the seed in the 'No-Soil' Compost in boxes in the greenhouse at a temperature of 65 degrees F. early in March. The seedlings will have to be pricked out into further boxes six weeks later – into a similar compost. Then after hardening the plants off in a frame it should be possible to put the plants out where they are to grow during the third week of May in rows 18 inches apart, giving 9 inches between the plants. I have produced Basil by sowing the seed in a frame early in April and thus grown the plants in the early stages in the frames under Dutch lights.

Basil should certainly be used with all pasta dishes – it should also be used in certain sauces for fish and a little can be mixed in with rice and with a dish of liver. We like it in sausage meat, it is grand in a tomato sauce over eggs while, of course, it is the essential herb in the Soupe au Pistou.

BERGAMOT (*Monarda didyma*)

This is a plant which can be grown if desired in the herbaceous border because it produces the most beautiful flowers. There are crimson, pink and mauvy varieties. The Bergamot is, in fact, the one exception to my inviolate rule of growing all the herbs in the narrow herb border. Both the leaves and the

* or upturned glass jam jars.

Herbs.

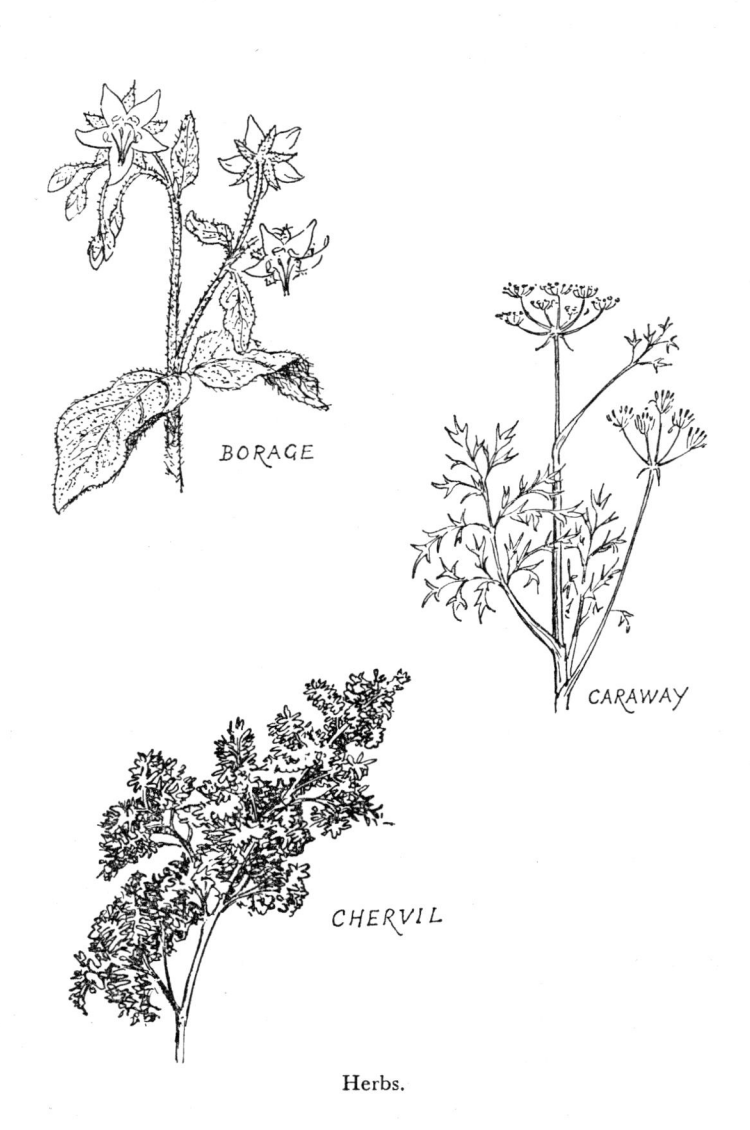

flowers of the Bergamot can be eaten and, in fact, the flower petals make the salad bowl look most attractive. Sometimes I use the red petals in conjunction with the blue flowers of the Borage which are also edible.

The Bergamot plants grow about 3 feet high and are happy in almost any type of soil. They suffer from blight in a dry year and then grow stunted; for this reason those who have a sandy or gravelly soil to cope with will do well to plant the various kinds of Bergamot in a shady spot. It also helps with any soil if plenty of fine organic matter like old compost is dug in before planting, as this helps to provide moisture during a dry summer period. In addition, sedge peat may be applied around the plants as a mulch to the depth of $\frac{1}{2}$ an inch or so.

There is no difficulty in propagating Bergamot, for each October or November the roots may be divided. I have left down clumps of Bergamot for four or five years but the clumps get rather large at the end of that period. The leaves are very useful indeed for making pot-pourri but their flavour tends to be rather strong and so only a soupçon should be used in a salad. One can add the flowers to lettuce in sandwiches and they give them a very pleasant flavour.

BORAGE *(Borango offcinalis)*

This is a plant that was probably introduced into Britain by the Romans because they used it in their wine cups. It is a very decorative herb and has always been associated with cheerfulness. Always plant it in the highest part of the herb bed so that the beautiful blue flowers, which tend to hang down, can be seen to the best advantage. The plant is sometimes biennial, but it is best grown as an annual in rows a foot apart. Sow the seeds in April and thin the seedlings out when they come through the ground, to 1 foot apart, six weeks later. It is one of the herbs that seeds itself very readily and after the first year there are always plenty of self-sown seedlings available to transplant into rows where desired.

Herbalists like the stalks and leaves of the Borage for throat and chest troubles because they are both rich in alkaline mucilage. Bees love the plant and visit the flowers regularly.

The young leaves can be used in salads to give a slight cucumber flavour. The older leaves can be used in soups and especially those such as bean and green pea. Boiled cabbage is much improved if it is served with a knob of butter on the top and this should be sprinkled with finely chopped Borage leaves just before serving.

As has already been suggested, the blue flowers can be used in salads to add colour, while claret cup, cider cup, lemonade and orangeade are much improved by the addition of the blue blossoms of Borage. Country folk use an infusion of the leaves to make Borage tea and this is said to be particularly cooling.

CHAMOMILE (*Anthemis nobilis*)

This is a herb that is not used in salads and stews and so is often omitted from the herb garden. It is a compact prostrate growing plant which will send out runners like a strawberry. Set the plants out in rows a foot apart and give 8 inches between the plants in the rows and there will be an almost continuous carpet at the end of the first year. In the gardens of Buckingham Palace I have seen a large Chamomile lawn, and when this is needed, the idea is to set the plants out 6 inches apart each way and then, when the lawn is established, mowing is done as for ordinary grass. The special strain grown for this purpose as Treneague.

The Chamomile is grown for its flowers and the harvesting usually takes place in July and August. The blossoms must be gathered without the stalks before there is any sign of brownness at the back of the flower head. White flowers give the best results.

These flower heads are used to make an infusion with which to wash fair hair. They can also be made into tea, four fresh flowers being sufficient per cup of boiling water. Chamomile tea is valuable in cases of insomnia, especially for old people.

CARAWAY (*Carum Carvi*)

This is another herb which could be omitted from the herb border because it is by no means as popular today as it was in our great-grandmother's time. She used the caraway seeds (they are really little fruits) to make delicious seed cake, seed-bread, seed-cheese. She also sprinkled the seeds on the top of roast pork, just before serving it, and gave a very light sprinkling to cabbage after putting on a knob of butter – this as an alternative to the sprinkling of Borage. It is, of course, the essential oil of the Caraway which is used in the liqueur called Kümmel.

The seeds may be sown in the autumn or spring in rows 2 feet apart, thinning out the plants to 18 inches apart in the rows. If the sowing is done in mid-September the plants will flower the following summer and the seeds can be gathered early that autumn. When, however, the seed sowing is delayed until the spring no harvesting can be done until the year afterwards. The moment the flowering is over the plants die down.

Cut the plants as soon as the seeds begin to ripen and before they are distributed all over the soil and are lost. Take the stems indoors, cover the heads with an old dust sheet and leave them in a warm room. After a fortnight or so, beat the sheet with a walking stick to thresh out the seeds as soon as they begin to loosen. After this lay the seeds out on a metal tray in the sun or dry them on the staging in the greenhouse. Drying could, of course, be done in a spare room indoors but the temperature must never be above 70 degrees F. When fully dried, store the seeds in an opaque jar fitted with a tight lid and they should be ready then to be used at any time of the year.

English Caraway seed is always considered to have the best flavour of any in Europe. They can be used as a flavouring for soups, for buns, for cake, and, of course, home-made sweets. In some parts of the country Caraway is put into bread.

CHERVIL (*Anthriscus cerefolium*)

This is a herb which should always be considered to have a subtler, more pleasant taste than parsley – it is, in fact, more spicy, though used for flavouring similar types of food. Because the flavour is so subtle and pleasant, it is usually used more generously than parsley.

It is an annual that is readily raised from seed and hates being transplanted. Sow the seeds therefore where the plants are to grow, 12 inches apart and then thin the plants out to 8 inches apart later. If you do try and transplant the seedlings even when they are young, they tend to flower immediately and so never produce enough leaves. Make one sowing in April and another sowing in July. Very often Chervil will seed itself in the row and then when the old plants have been pulled up the young plants will grow on in their place.

Some womenfolk are so keen on Chervil that they sow seeds in boxes or pots filled with the ' No-Soil ' Compost in September. Then by keeping the pots or boxes in the greenhouse they can have their Chervil leaves during the winter months. Others have sown the seed about the third week of August under cloches and then have grown the Chervil under these miniature greenhouses without any difficulty throughout the winter.

The leaves of Chervil can be used in the salad bowl, green and fresh. As the foliage fades, it turns to a lovely shade of pink, and some therefore use the leaves in this stage to give colour to a mixed bowl of salad. Chervil, when chopped fine, can be added with sliced lemon as a nice finish to iced tomato soup. When dried it is an excellent fines herbes for adding to egg, chicken and cheese dishes. It is delicious when chopped up fresh and added to a potato or cucumber salad. When the leaves are dried and powdered they can be used to add a piquant flavour to a stew.

CHIVES (*Allium schoenoprasum*)

This hardy perennial has been mentioned briefly in Chapter II; it can, however, be grown, if desired, in the herb border and the leaves, or ' grass ' as some people call it, are gathered or cut whenever they are needed. The rows should be renewed every third year, the clumps being divided in March for planting in rows a foot apart and allowing six inches between the plants. If mauve flowers appear they should be cut off the moment they show. Those who find it difficult to buy plants may sow seeds early in April.

Chives are used to provide an oniony flavour to omelettes, soups, stews and other meat dishes; when chopped up finely they are sometimes added to mashed potatoes.

DILL (*Anethum graveolens*)

Just as Chervil has been described as subtler than parsley, so Dill has been thought of as a pleasing type of Caraway. It is one of the quickest plants to grow as an annual and for years was much used in water to soothe babies and children to sleep.

Sow the seed early in April in a sunny situation, making the drills a foot apart and ½ an inch deep. Extremely thin sowing must be carried out because when the plants come through they need to be thinned to 8 inches apart. The plants, when growing, look rather like Fennel though they are definitely more compact. They may grow to a height of 3 feet.

The Dill foliage when chopped up fresh gives a lovely new flavour to cucumber sandwiches. In Sweden – Dill is used with boiled lamb and with fish. In Norway the leaves are used as well as mint with new potatoes. In Great Britain the leaves are cut up finely and distributed evenly throughout a salad and guests never discover what the delicious flavour is. Fresh sprigs of Dill added to a halibut and salmon, before serving, do something for these dishes. Fresh Dill chopped finely may be added to scrambled eggs or mashed potatoes. In France I have eaten pickled Dill and found it delicious. In Germany they add Dill to Sauerkraut.

We have made Dill vinegar by putting the so-called seeds, which are really little fruits, into fresh vinegar for a fortnight or so when it adds a delicious flavour. Dill vinegar can then be used for pickling gherkins or little cucumbers.

FENNEL

Garden Fennel	(*Foeniculum offcinale*)
Common Fennel	(*Foeniculum vulgare*)
Sweet Fennel	(*Foeniculum dulce*) (sometimes called Florence Fennel or Finocchio)

One of the important things is never to confuse the Common Fennel and the Garden Fennel. The Common Fennel is the wild plant found in the hedgerows; the Garden Fennel, on the other hand, produces a bigger plant on the whole with leaf stalks that form sheafs around the base. Big plants of Fennel may grow to a height of 6 feet and cover an area of 3 square feet. The Fennel is a perennial and can, for this reason, be left in the border for five or six years. The plants produce a mass of fine, feathery leaves, green in colour, though there are some strains which seem to produce a bronze foliage. The flowers are yellow and they seed quickly. One of the problems of growing Fennel in a herb bed, is that the seeds are easily distributed, and so little seedlings may be found all over the garden. These want watching because they have long tap roots and unless they are eliminated quickly, if may be difficult to get rid of them.

If the Fennel seeds are not required for flavouring, then it is as well to remove the flowers the moment they appear. In fact, in most cases where the young stems are used, the plants should be kept cut back and this results (a) in plenty of tender shoots and (b) in no flowering.

The seeds should be sown about the middle of April in drills 2 feet apart and the plants thinned to 15 inches apart in the rows. By keeping the plants cut back they can be made to conform to this standardised regime. In fact, those who like Fennel as a substitute for celery, often earth up some of the plants and then when the stems are blanched they cook them.

I always think that the flavour of Fennel is a somewhat queer mixture of aniseed and liquorice; the leaves can be picked off at any time of the year and be cut up finely before being added to lettuce or any other green salad. Tender stems may be cut when they are 6 inches high and these may be put into the salad bowl when peeled. Fennel is especially useful with the oily types of fish, like salmon and mackerel, and may either be served as a sauce with these dishes or may be powdered and rubbed inside the fishes before they are cooked. In Norway and Sweden fresh Fennel is served as a garnish to many dishes.

The Finnochio mentioned in the introduction is, of course, the Florence Fennel and is a much smaller plant altogether. Swellings occur where the bases of the leaf stalk overlap and these swellings are earthed up like celery. They are boiled and served with a white sauce or they can be cooked in the Italian way – that is, stewed in a stock made from bones.

MARJORAM

Pot Marjoram (*Origanum onites*)
Sweet Marjoram (*Origanum marjorana*) (sometimes called Knotted Marjoram)
Wild Marjoram (*Origanum vulgare*)

Of course, the Wild Marjoram, which is commonly found in the South and particularly in Kent and other counties where chalk is present, can be used as a herb in the kitchen but it really has not got as good a flavour as the cultivated types. The Sweet Marjoram is tender and is always treated as an annual; the Pot Marjoram, on the other hand, is hardy and is grown as a perennial.

The Pot Marjoram can be easily propagated by cutting off rooted shoots from the old plants in late October and early November and planting them out 1 foot square. This is a herb that needs plenty of water in the summer, for if the plants are allowed to get dry the leaves turn bright yellow and may be covered with spots. Water well, if necessary, and then cover the ground with sedge peat an inch deep. Always harvest Marjoram when the flower buds are first seen in July – it's only possible to get one good harvesting a year for the dried leaves. (See Chapter VI.) The leaves of the Knotted Marjoram have a far more aromatic flavour than those of the Pot Marjoram. Some cooks mix these two Marjorams together in equal parts and claim that they get better flavour as a result.

Dried Marjoram can be mixed with other herbs to which it gives a flavour of nutmeg. This is the powdered dried herb that is used by the Italians in Pizza Pie. It is called by the Italians and Spaniards, Oregano. Dried Marjoram can be used as a flavouring for omelettes and scrambled eggs while fresh Marjoram is delicious with cheese as a filling for brown bread sandwiches. I use a sprinkle of Marjoram in soups and stews and my wife always adds it to her pot-pourris.

MINT

Lamb Mint	(*Mentha viridis (spicata)*)
Round-Leaved Mint	(*Mentha rotundifolia*)
Hairy Mint	(*Mentha sylvestris*)
Middlesex Mint	(*Mentha villoso-nervata*)
Phillips Mint	(*Mentha cordifolia*)
East Anglian Mint	(*Mentha niliaca var. alopecuroides*)

There are, as the heading shows, a very large number of mints used in this country today. The leading authorities on the subject agree that there are at least six distinct forms, mainly hybrids. Generally speaking I find that *Mentha spicata*, sometimes called Spearmint, is the one that is invariably used for mint sauce; it produces long narrow leaves and nice stiff stems. It is hardy, but unfortunately is liable to attacks of the mint rust disease.

The Hairy Mint is earlier than the Spearmint, but (a) it never looks as attractive and (b) the flavour is poor. Its great advantage, however, is that it does not get the rust disease badly. The Middlesex Mint is a hybrid between the Lamb Mint and Hairy Mint. It has red tinged stems and shorter, broader leaves.

The Round-Leaved Mint is known as the apple scented or apple mint, but as the leaves are extremely hairy they are not usually liked by women. Epicures, however, say that it makes the best type of mint sauce. Phillips Mint is a hybrid between the Round-Leaved Mint and the Lamb Mint. It is a vigorous grower, has rounded leaves and grows a rather coarse plant on the whole. Gardeners like it, however, because it goes on producing fresh young shoots until well on in November and it is seldom infected with rust.

The East Anglian Mint is the tallest of the group. It may grow to a height of 6 feet. It produces wrinkled woolly leaves, which are resistant to rust and it makes first-class mint sauce. Most people, however, consider it too tall for the normal garden.

On the whole, mint prefers a rich soil which is weed free. Don't make the mistake of thinking that it prefers to be in the shade because when the plants lack sun they make long internodes and very few leaves in consequence. Mint is a great robber and therefore it pays to be generous with well rotted compost when preparing the bed. Dig in the compost, 1 large bucketful to the square yard and add a fish manure in addition at 3 ounces to the square yard. Never leave a mint bed down longer than 3 years. The Author's plan is to make a small new bed every year and, in addition, to give the older beds a top dressing of compost each autumn.

There is never any difficulty in planting up a new bed in the late autumn or early spring. Small pieces of the underground runners are used, 2 inches long, and these are planted in drills 2 inches deep and in rows 2 feet apart. It is not long before the mint spreads in between the rows, but if it overruns the land allotted to it, it may be cut back with a sharp spade. Chopping back of mint in this way seems to do the plants good rather than harm.

Keep down mint rust by burning off the tops in late September or early October, dry straw being laid among the stems for this purpose. A quick fire is needed, so that the stems may be burnt without injuring the roots below. Another method is to cut the tops down in October and put them on the compost heap and then water the bed with a 5 per cent solution of a neutral high boiling tar oil wash. This can be bought from any good horticultural chemist.

Mint roots may be dug up for planting in boxes in October and if these are taken into the greenhouse, nice young plants will be available during the winter time for flavouring purposes.

Fresh mint leaves may be used in a salad and they give a nice fresh flavour which makes all the difference. A sprig of mint should always be put into the saucepan when cooking new potatoes or green peas. When the leaves are chopped up fine and mixed with vinegar a delicious mint sauce is made. Pour a little boiling water over the finely cut fresh leaves just to wet them and finally pour over the vinegar and leave to stand for four hours before using. Mint sauce made in this way is quite different! Some people prefer to use a mint jelly with mutton and lamb. Mint tea is a good cure for indigestion, while some like mint drinks with meals.

An excellent salad can be made with onions or chives, grated raw carrots, grated Hamburg parsley and cut mint leaves. The onions must be sliced finely and after mixing with the grated roots, the chopped mint should be added. Season with salt and pepper, and serve. Incidentally, perhaps the best mint sauce is made from a mixture of *M. niliaca* and *M. spicata*.

PARSLEY (*Carum petroselinum*)

There is more superstition about parsley than probably about any other herb. In Suffolk, for instance, they insist that to get the best results the seed must be sown on Good Friday. In Cornwall, it is thought unlucky to give away parsley plants as, indeed, it is in France. In the Southern States of America, it is said that parsley seed goes seven times to the Devil and back before it germinates and that is why it is so slow coming up.

There are two main types of parsley, the plain leaved and the moss curled. The latter is the most popular but the former is hardier and stands up to wet weather and frost better. My experience, therefore, is that it is better to grow the plain leaved or firm leaved parsley in the North and the curled types in the South. As has already been suggested, parsley seed takes a long time to germinate and it is often two months before the little seedlings are seen. It is important, therefore, to sow early in April and again early in August and to thin the seedlings the moment they are through, to 6 inches apart. This gives the plants a chance of growing properly.

Parsley does well as an edging plant and may therefore either be grown in the herb border or around the edge of the vegetable garden. (An aunt of mine would always insist on growing it as an edging to a rose bed!) It is a plant that is happy in semi-shade and it is rather partial to a dampish position; it seems to revel in organic forms of nitrogen and thus when the plants are half-grown, old soot may be given at a handful to the yard run or dried blood at 2 ounces to the yard run. Everything should be done to prevent flower stalks from developing and the moment these are seen they should be cut down almost to soil level.

The soil where parsley is to be grown should be forked over in order to incorporate well rotted compost at the rate of one 2-gallon bucketful to the square yard. In addition, it pays to rake in fine sedge peat into the top inch or so at half a bucketful to the square yard. If the soil is sandy and the weather dry, damp the sedge peat thoroughly first. A fish manure with a 10 per cent potash content should be applied at 4 ounces to the square yard so that it can be raked in with the peat. Finally, when the strip of ground has been trodden and raked level, the ground should be dressed with carbonate of lime at 6 ounces to the square yard.

The seed may be sown in April and again in August as has been suggested, the drills being $\frac{1}{2}$ an inch deep and 15 inches apart. It is tremendously important to try and sow the seeds so that they are no thicker than about an inch apart in the drill. The best way of doing this is to mix the seeds with 5 times their bulk of sand. If you want to produce really large succulent plants, the thin sowing must be followed by early thinning. Cover the August sowings with cloches (see Chapter III) so as to keep the plants growing throughout the winter.

Those who have not got cloches should dig up one or two plants in the middle of September and pot them up into 6-inch pots using the 'No-Soil' Potting Compost. The pots should then either be placed in a deep frame where the plants can be kept frost free or may be placed on the staging of a cool greenhouse. I have often seen a pot of parsley on a shelf in the kitchen near the light in country cottages.

People who complain that the leaves of parsley are gritty and that they have to be well washed in consequence before using or drying, should apply plenty of sedge peat alongside the rows as a mulch, for this will keep the leaves perfectly clean.

Parsley is, of course, used as a decoration with cold meat, it's delicious when cut up and served cold with a salad, it gives the perfect flavour to an omelette, it's used for parsley sauces and probably it is the most important of all the herbs used in British cooking.

PURSLANE
Green Purslane   (*Portulaca oleracea*)
Golden Purslane   (*Portulaca sativa*)

As the heading shows there are two main kinds of Purslane,

the Green, often known as the True Purslane, and its Golden counterpart. The real Purslane has much thicker fleshy leaves than the Golden, but the latter is much liked because it looks well in the salad bowl. Unfortunately, Golden Purslane is not as hardy as the green type. Both of them, however, like positions in the full sun and they are grown as tender, half-hardy annuals. (Unfortunately, it is not always easy to get the seed of the Golden Purslane.)

When preparing the strip of ground where the seeds are to be sown, work in sedge peat or really fine sifted compost at the rate of one bucketful to the square yard. In addition, add a fish manure with a 6 per cent potash content at 4 ounces to the square yard. The organic matter is usually badly needed because Purslane suffers in times of drought, but when there is plenty of humus in the soil it can keep going. The soil must not be acid and when there is any doubt about this, carbonate of lime should be applied as a top dressing at 5 to 6 ounces to the square yard – after the bed has been prepared and firmed.

Sow the seed about the beginning of May in rows a foot apart and thin the seedlings out to 6 inches apart when they are one inch high. To obtain succession make a second sowing a month later and if necessary, even a third sowing a month after that.

The plants must never be allowed to grow long and leggy nor to flower and go to seed. Keep the leaves cut regularly. There should be no difficulty in getting four good crops of leaves from each plant. Pick these leaves with their stalks but before putting the foliage into salads remove them. Purslane gives a very pleasant flavour to the salad bowl and is first-class when made into sandwiches.

SAGE (*Salvia offcinalis*)

There is little doubt that the Romans introduced sage into Great Britain for they used it as a stuffing for the richer meats like pork and wild duck. Many British housewives find the flavour of sage too strong and they tell me that it is a herb that does not blend well with others. Enormous quantities of sage are, however, used every year in sausage making while small quantities of powdery, dried sage can be added with great success to soups, dumplings, to cream cheese, especially when used in sandwiches.

Unfortunately, all kinds of types of sages are found in gardens and the reason probably is because the plants 'sport' so readily. There are broad-leafed sages, variegated sages, narrow-leafed sages, as well as those with white, pink, and even blue flowers. Some of the flowering forms look extremely attractive when used in a salad bowl and I have met with all kinds and types which seem to have a similar delicious flavour. Generally speaking, however, it is best to stick to the broad-leafed form and to renew the plants every four or five years. If you do not do this, the plants are apt to grow tall and straggly.

Sage prefers a light, well drained soil and a sunny, open situation. It is usually propagated by means of cuttings and most gardeners pull off rooted pieces of old plants for this purpose. Three-year-old bushes are earthed up or, as an alternative, the centres of the plants are filled up with the 'No-Soil' Compost. If this is done in May, the lower parts of the stems of the plants will have grown roots in a couple of months and they can then be severed from the parent and put out on their own. In the south some people do this earthing up in March and the severing in May or early June.

It is always better to propagate from the specimens in the border that have the least tendency to flower and thus gradually as a result you will build up a non-flowering strain. Choose also the types with the broadest leaves on each occasion.

Those who want to make a start by sowing seed, should do this early in the month of May, the idea being to sow the seeds thinly in drills ¾-inch deep and 9 inches apart. The seedlings should be thinned out to 9 inches apart in the row when they are 1 inch high. Finally, the plants should stand at 18 inches by 18 inches.

The young stems of the sage are cut in June and again early in September. After the first harvesting an application of fish manure should be given at 4 ounces to the square yard and this should be lightly hoed in. See that the fish manure does not rest on the leaves of the plants or it may scorch them.

Normally, the sage leaves will be gathered and dried as

described in Chapter VI. When they are dried and powdery they can, of course, be used in a sage and onion stuffing, or mixed in with a cream cheese. It is possible, however, to use fresh sage leaves in salads providing this is not overdone, and to use them also as a flavouring in lettuce sandwiches. Country-folk often make sage tea and say that this is very good for stomach troubles.

SAVORY
Sweet Savory (*Satureia hortensis*)
Winter Savory (*Satureia montana*)

The winter savory is a perennial and I never have had any difficulty in over-wintering it in the south. Even in the north it will usually live through the winter if the soil is not too heavy. The summer savory is an annual and should be cut before the plants come into flower; it is then that the leaves are ready for drying.

The soil for summer Savory should be prepared as advised for Parsley. Sow the seed in drills 1 foot apart and $\frac{1}{2}$-inch deep. Mix the seed with an equal quantity of sand or powdered sedge peat, so that the sowing is done really thinly. When the seedlings come through the ground, thin them out to 9 inches apart and bushy plants will be formed about 1 foot in height. Winter Savory may be propagated by taking cuttings from the plants in the spring and striking them in sandy soil in a frame, in a sandy compost in boxes in the greenhouse or out-of-doors under cloches. Sometimes it is possible to pull off rooted portions from the base of the plants. In either case the rows should be 2 foot apart with the plants set out 18 inches apart in the rows. For this choose a sunny situation.

The cutting or harvesting should be done twice in the season, usually June and September, so as to prevent the bushes becoming woody. If you cut twice a year in this way it is possible to leave the plants in position for six years.

The flavour of savory is very much like that of thyme but somewhat sharper. The leaves should be dried as described in the next chapter and then, when they are powdered, they may be added to the mixed herbs. I use fresh leaves in the water in

c*

Herbs.

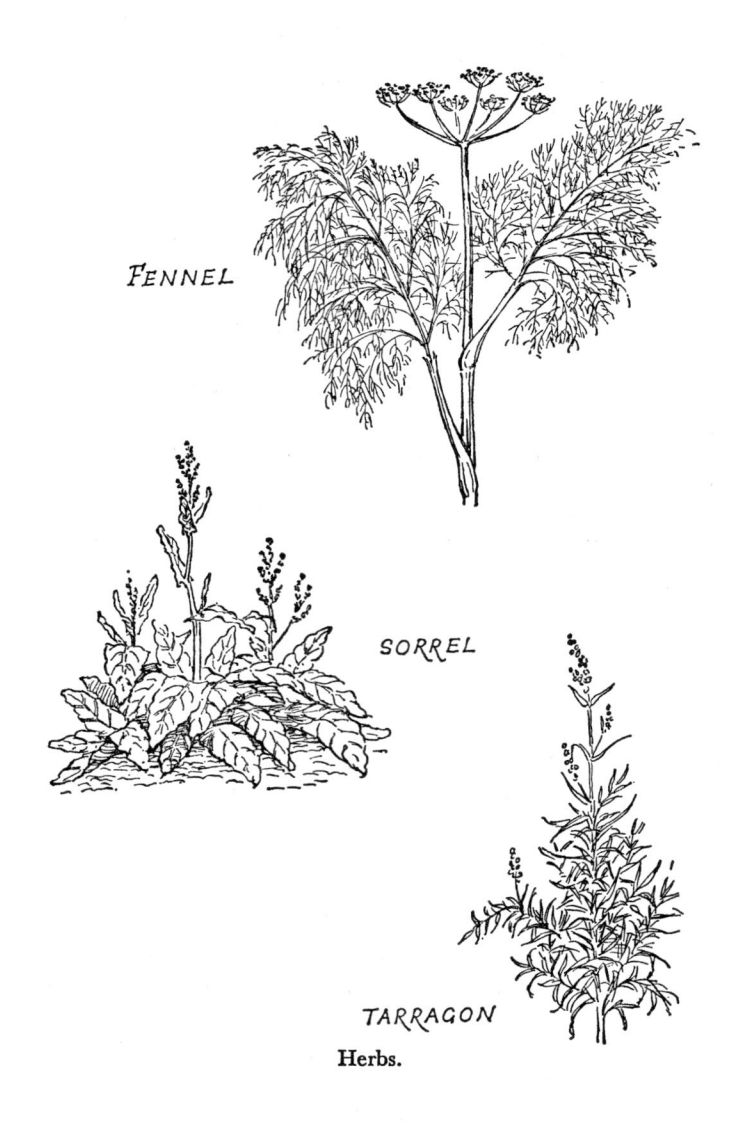

which broad beans are boiled rather in the way that you add mint to the water for early potatoes. The alternative is to make a white sauce for pouring over the broad beans and the Savory leaves should be used as the flavouring.

SORREL
Garden Sorrel (*Rumex acetosa*)
French Sorrel (*Rumex scutatus*)

Sorrel is often found growing wild in fields and gardens, and I know many a lawn which has far too much sorrel in it! It is a plant that loves acid soil and is invariably propagated by seed sowing. The French Sorrel prefers a dry sandy situation and the true Garden Sorrel, a dampish situation. The former variety is more popular with chefs because it is not so acid. In both cases it is a good idea to prepare the ground by forking in sedge peat lightly at 1 bucketful to the square yard. In addition, a balanced fish fertiliser should be used at 9 ounces to the square yard. No lime should be given because the plant prefers an acid soil. The seed should be sown thinly in drills 1 foot apart and the seedlings thinned out later to 6 inches apart in the rows.

The French Sorrel, with its broad fleshy leaves can be used when cut up in salads and is very delicious indeed. We often put fresh sorrel leaves into soups and stews and the flavouring given is most unusual. The leaves are never dried but are invariably used fresh.

SWEET CICELY (*Myrrhis odorata*)

As I travel over Great Britain I find this plant given a number of different names. It has been called Sweet Fern, Sweet Chervil, Cow Chervil and Cow Fern. It is a very attractive herb and I have had it growing in the herb border 5 foot high. The leaves are silky and soft to the touch and they have a slight aniseed flavour about them. They are much sweeter, however, than the normal aniseed.

The plants are very slow growers and I have known gardeners complain to me that at the end of the first season the specimens are only six or seven inches high. There is nothing to worry about, however, for the leaves will die down in the winter and in the spring they will appear again and gradually the plants will increase in height.

The plants like to be grown in full sun and they prefer a light soil to a heavy one. The seed should be sown in April in the south and in May in the north, in drills 1 foot apart and 1 inch deep. In the first year the thinning should be done to 4 inches apart but the following spring a second thinning should be done to a foot apart. Some gardeners dig up the plants in April of the second season in order to be able to plant them out 2 feet square.

It is seldom that the leaves of Sweet Cicely are dried, they are generally used fresh and if they are picked young and are cut up a little, they make a welcome addition to the salad bowl to which they give a spicy and quite distinctive flavour. They can also be used by those who like a soupçon of aniseed in sandwiches.

TARRAGON (*Artemisia dracunculus*)

This is a perennial plant of a shrub-like habit of growth. It insists on a really well drained situation and prefers a light sandy soil to a heavy clay. It should never be planted in heavily manured rich land for then it tends to make plenty of soft growth late in the year which invariably gets killed by the frost.

There are two types of tarragon. The French and the Russian. The former should always be grown, for the latter is quite useless in the kitchen. The leaves should be cut early in July in the south and late July in the north, i.e. just before flowering. It is usually possible to make a second cut at the beginning of September.

Propagation is carried out in two ways: (1) by the division of plants in April or (2) by the pulling off of young shoots in May and pushing them into a mixture of coarse silver sand and sedge peat in a frame. On the whole the cuttings root fairly easily and they have been struck by dibbling them into sandy soil in the open. When rooted, the cuttings should be planted in rows a foot apart, allowing one foot apart also in the rows.

Tarragon is used almost entirely for making tarragon vinegar; the method is a simple one. Plenty of fresh leaves are steeped in a quantity of white vinegar for at least 14 days; after the vinegar has absorbed the flavour of the tarragon, it should be re-bottled and firmly corked. It can then be used as required afterwards. The leaves can be picked off in July or September, as has already been suggested, and these can be dried as detailed in Chapter VI. The powdered tarragon can then be used in stews, and it makes an excellent sauce for fish. Friends of mine usually put a few fresh tarragon leaves in a salad and they provide a rather hot but unusual flavour. Tarragon can also be added to melted butter for putting over a fillet steak or over vegetables. Tarragon is excellent in an omelette and it makes a first-class dressing for chicken. Many people use it also as a seasoning for lamb and mutton. Tarragon vinegar is the base for Sauce Bernaise.

THYME (*Thymus vulgaris*)

Thyme is one of the well-known herbs which comes to us from the Mediterranean region. It does best in a soil where there is plenty of lime and is the traditional herb for jugged hare.

There is Common Thyme sometimes called Black Thyme, and Lemon Thyme. The Common Thyme is divided into two sub-divisions (a) the English Thyme with green broadish leaves and (b) the French Thyme with narrow, grey leaves with a strong smell of camphor to them. Lemon Thyme is similar to the Common Thyme, except that the leaves are lighter in colour and they have a lemon-ny smell about them. In addition there are the Golden Thymes and the Ornamental Thymes, such as are used in the Rock Garden and in between crazy paving.

Choose a really well-drained sunny position for any of the thymes. Remember they come from the Mediterranean and this gives the clue to their treatment. They love sunshine, they can put up with droughty conditions and they don't mind a sandy or gravelly light soil. Lime is a necessity and if the B.D.H. Soil Indicator is used to test a sample and this reveals acidity, carbonate of lime should be applied at anything from

4 to 7 ounces per square yard. The soil indicating fluid will reveal the quantity needed.

Thyme should be planted in rows 2 feet apart allowing 18 inches between the plants. Renewal is desirable every third or fourth year. Few plants are easier to increase than Thyme and thus there is no reason to allow plants to grow old and untidy. You can dig them up and replant them deeply, even if you have to double the roots up, and this doesn't seem to make any difference, the plants go on growing.

It is possible to increase by taking cuttings, or by causing the lower branches to root as advised in the case of Sage. The ordinary Thyme can be raised from seed but not the Lemon Thyme. By the way, those who decide to divide roots should always do so during the month of March.

Cut the Thyme twice a year : (a) at the end of May before the flowers open and (b) about the middle of August. Always take a pair of shears and cut the plants down whether the herbs are needed at that moment or no. If this is not done, the plants get long and lanky. By pruning my Thyme rows back twice a year in this way, I am able to keep them going for six years without having to dig up and replant. It helps, of course, if a fish manure with a 6 per cent potash content is given at 4 to 5 ounces to the yard, run down the side of the rows each September.

The little leaves of Lemon Thyme may be used fresh in salads and give a delicious flavour. Chopped fine, they may be sprinkled on cut fresh tomatoes with great success. Thyme is usually dried, however, before being used, and is often rubbed through a coarse sieve afterwards. It keeps well and can be used as desired. It is, however, very powerful and should not be overdone. It is a must in Bouquet Garni, it is first-class in cheese dishes, it is good with mutton and pork and fine powdered thyme may be rubbed into the flesh of poultry. It is absolutely first-class with Red Mullet. It is, of course, one of the many herbs used in Benedictine.

MISCELLANEOUS

There are one or two herbs used in the kitchen which have

purposely not been included, for one reason or another. Rosemary is one, the leaves of which have a dominant gingery flavour to them. They are sometimes used as a part of a stuffing for game, large fish or lamb. Rosemary, however, is a shrub and should be grown in the shrub border.

The leaves of the Bay tree are also used, either dried or fresh; in fact, when dried they are part of the perfect Bouquet Garni. My Mother used to use fresh leaves when preparing soused mackerel. If a fresh leaf is laid on a mutton chop while it is being grilled, it gives it a lovely aromatic flavour. Some people like dried and powdered bay leaves in milk puddings, cornflour shapes and custards.

Some people like to serve Rosemary leaves with lamb or mutton, while a friend of the author always cooks a veal fillet or chop with a bay leaf on top.

CHAPTER VI

THE PREPARATION AND DRYING OF HERBS

HERBS may be dried satisfactorily in any normal home. It is only necessary to take a little trouble and to see that during the slow drying process the herbs are not covered with dust. It is worth while, therefore, covering the leaves while they are in the drying trays with a large piece of clean, butter muslin.

Always harvest the leaves early in the morning on a nice dry day. Do the picking just after the dew has gone and before the sun is too hot. In most cases the harvesting should take place just as the plants are about to flower, for it is then that they are at their best. There are, of course, exceptions to this rule as in the case of Parsley. Where herbs have very small leaves, the stems should be cut, leaves and all, and where the foliage is really large, individual leaves can be picked off.

Having harvested, wash the leaves thoroughly and in the case of those with smaller leaves, while they are still on their stems. Then tie the stems together in convenient bunches and hang them up in the kitchen to dry. During this time they should be covered with butter muslin bags. Individual leaves, without stems, may be laid on wire trays and it is these that are covered with the strips of butter muslin. All drying should be done slowly. If you are determined to devote a day to herb drying, the plan will be to strip the leaves off the herbs and lay them out individually on small baking trays and then put them in the oven with the door open, or if you have an Aga, some of the ovens of which are very hot, even put the trays on a chair or stool just outside the oven, so that they merely receive the hot air.

Another reason for drying the herbs in a muslin bag or covered with butter muslin, is that it tends to keep them in the dark and so a better colour is preserved. When the leaves are really dry there is no difficulty in stripping them off the stems for they should then be quite crisp. If they are not crisp and do not come away easily you will know that they must be dried some more.

Now comes the crushing on a flat board or enamel-topped table, by giving them a good rolling with a rolling pin and then by sieving them through a fine wire sieve. When they are like a powder they should be stored in a glass bottle with a plastic screw top and this having been labelled with the name of the herb, should be wrapped around with blue paper for this is the best way of preserving the colour.

Herbs with larger leaves, like Parsley and Mint, should be picked off their stalks and washed; they should then be tied up in a length of butter muslin to form a ball about the size of a coconut. This should then be dipped into a solution of bicarbonate of soda, which must be boiling at the time. The formula is a $\frac{1}{4}$ ounce of bicarbonate of soda to 2 quarts of water. This dipping, curiously enough, is called by the chef – blanching, and is done to preserve the green colour in the leaves of the herbs.

After this short blanching process, which need not take more than a minute, the leaves should be drained for a few minutes and then should be spread out on a butter-muslin covered tray for placing in a cool oven at a temperature of 120 degrees F. As I have already said, if the oven should be at a higher temperature than this, place the herbs on their trays in front of the oven with the door open, so that they receive the hot air. If it is possible to keep the temperature constant at 120 degrees F. and no more, it is possible to have the herb leaves prepared, dry in just over the hour. Some people place metal trays above a gas or electric stove, and when herbs are treated in this way the drying process often takes four hours. Once again, may it be emphasised, that slow drying is far preferable to quick drying.

Once the larger leaves are crisp and dry they should be crushed to powder as advised in the case of the smaller leaves like thyme. They should then be stored in bottles, lightly stoppered and covered with dark paper to prevent the light getting at them. The author has kept dried parsley for over a year in this way and at the end of the time it has still retained its lovely green colour. To get the best results the herbs should be stored separately and the mixing should be done at the time of use. Those who cannot be bothered with doing this, may store the herbs already mixed, and a very good bouquet consists of 1 part by weight of thyme and 1 part by weight Sweet Marjoram, 1 part by weight Winter Savoy and 2 parts by weight of Parsley.

Other leaves may be dried in a similar manner, like for instance, those of the Bay tree, mentioned at the close of the previous chapter. The leaves of Dill are dried for use in pickles; Nasturtium seeds are dried and when these are ready they are stored in bottles of white vinegar and prove to be quite a good substitute for capers. For each half pint of white vinegar add 1 Bay leaf, 3 black peppercorns and a $\frac{1}{4}$ ounce of rock salt.

SOME USEFUL RECIPES INVOLVING HERBS

Sauces

There are a number of sauces that entail the use of herbs and they are far more delicious when you use the herbs grown in your garden on soil high in humus than when made from any old herbs bought in the shop.

Fennel Sauce

1 tablespoonful of dried fennel	1 oz. fresh butter
1 dessertspoonful of white cane sugar	$\frac{3}{4}$ oz. white flour
1 tablespoonful of white vinegar	Yolk of 1 egg
$\frac{1}{2}$ pint of fish stock	

Melt the butter slowly in a saucepan and stir in the flour slowly, then add the stock, continuing to stir the whole time and bring slowly to the boil. Simmer for five minutes and then remove the saucepan from the source of heat and add the vinegar slowly, stirring continuously. Then add the sugar and stir this in well and, finally, the fennel. Dust with a little pepper and salt, then put the saucepan back on the heat but do not boil and while it is heating up again add a little of the sauce to the yolk of egg, which must be beaten well first. Now add the beaten egg and sauce to the saucepan and re-heat before serving.

Bechamel Sauce

1 pint rich milk	1 stalk of celery cut into pieces
1 small shallot	2 oz. fresh butter
1 piece of carrot, the size of a walnut	2 oz. white flour
	1 teaspoonful of Bouquet Garni
8 peppercorns	Salt and pepper to taste

Put the milk, peppercorns and the vegetables, when sliced, into a saucepan and bring to the boil slowly. Add the Bouquet Garni after the first five minutes and then when the milk is boiling, cover with a saucepan lid and place on the side of the stove to infuse for half-an-hour. Now strain carefully through a fine strainer into a warm bowl. Put some of the liquid in another warm bowl and add the flour slowly, stirring to make a paste. Heat the butter and pour this in, stirring all the time. Now add the creamed flour and butter to the liquid in the other bowl and return to the saucepan. Heat slowly once more and add the pepper and salt. Some people who want to make a very rich sauce add $\frac{3}{4}$ of a pint of cream at this time. It takes about 40 minutes to make this sauce!

Sauce Bernaise

1 gill tarragon vinegar	3 yolks of egg
1 teaspoonful chopped tarragon leaves	1 crushed clove of garlic
1 teaspoonful chopped chervil leaves	2 oz. fresh butter
2 small shallots, finely chopped	Salt and pepper to taste

Put the herbs, garlic, shallots, salt and pepper in the vinegar and bring slowly to the boil. Keep boiling slowly until the quantity is reduced by about a half. Put through a strainer into a warmed bowl and cool. Now put the yolks of egg into a small saucepan and stir in the strained vinegar, keeping the heat low. Add the butter a little at a time and the consistency should become thick and smooth, like mayonnaise. The secret is never to allow the sauce to boil and for this reason it is a good thing to do the work in a double saucepan. Just before the sauce is to be served, stir in a pinch of powdered tarragon and an equal pinch of dried parsley. This is an excellent sauce to serve with grilled steak, grilled lobster and grilled kidney.

Bouquet Garni

This, in the Victorian days, consisted of two sprigs of parsley, one bay leaf, one sprig of thyme, one sprig of marjoram, one sprig of basil, and a blade of mace. These were tied together in a little bouquet and were used for flavouring. Chefs always reserved the right to omit some of the herbs and add others and the secret of the flavour of dishes was, in fact, in their hands.

Today, the Bouquet Garni usually consists of the herbs that have been mentioned in the list, mixed together after drying but omitting the mace. In modern parlance, adding a pinch of mixed herbs, is the 1970's counterpart to the placing of the Bouquet Garni in the saucepan as the sauces were being prepared.

Soupe Au Pistou

This was the soup my wife and I discovered in Corsica and which is also popular in some parts of Sardinia.

2 quarts of water	2 baby marrows (no longer than 6 inches each)
½ lb. French beans	
6 small new potatoes	3 oz. short-length spaghetti
½ lb. freshly-shelled green peas	Salt and pepper to taste
3 medium-sized carrots	

Cut the French beans into short lengths, wash and quarter the new potatoes, cut the carrots into rounds, cut the baby marrows into inch-thick slices, unskinned, and add all these to the water, together with the salt and pepper. Cook slowly until the vegetables are nearly ready and 15 minutes before the vegetables are completely cooked, add the spaghetti.

While this is going on – prepare the Pistou : take 12 fresh basil leaves, ¼ lb. of grated cheese, hard gruyère is good, 3 tablespoonfuls of olive oil and 3 small cloves of garlic when peeled. Put these ingredients, when cut up, into a mortar, and pound them together with a pestle until a smooth paste has been produced. A little more salad oil may be added if necessary. Two minutes before taking the soup to the table add the Pistou, stirring well, but do not let it boil. Serve the soup in bowls and provide your guests with a little grated parmesan to sprinkle over the top.

Courgettes with Tarragon

A few years ago you couldn't sell courgettes in Great Britain, and now they are very popular. Actually, of course, they are just small marrows.

4 courgettes	1 tablespoon tarragon
1½ oz. fresh butter	4 peppercorns
1 pint water	1 small fresh green pepper, if possible
1 teaspoonful salt	

Remove the little stems from the ends of the courgettes and then cook them in the salted water which should be brought to the boil first. They usually take about 5 minutes. Now cut the courgettes into thick slices, after draining them, melt the butter slowly in another small saucepan and add the powdered tarragon, pepper and salt. Toss the sliced courgettes into the melted butter and cook till tender. Serve them while they are still crisp and hot. Just before putting them on the table, sprinkle with the finely chopped green pepper which you bought specially for the purpose.

CHAPTER VII

THE CABBAGE FAMILY AS SALADS

YEARS ago people would have found it very astonishing to find the hearts of cabbages in a salad. Even today there are men and women who can only eat a cabbage when it has been boiled for a long time and is served up hot and soggy. We are a curious nation from the point of view of our boiled potatoes and our boiled cabbage! Actually, almost all members of the cabbage family are delicious when used raw in the salad bowl.

Few people are sufficiently salad minded and that is one of the reasons why this book is written, for during the summer period there is far too much stretching forth of hands to the eternal lettuce and varying it perhaps with the tomato and the cucumber. It is an interesting fact and one which few people believe – but the tomato itself has only been really popular in the last thirty years!

If you have travelled abroad, however, and many more people are doing this today, you will know what lovely salads there can be. I can think of lovely cabbage salad made with crisp, fresh hearts of cabbages, shredded finely and mixed with a little apple, some banana and a small quantity of orange segments. What joy this was when eaten with cream cheese and chopped nuts and dressed with a special mayonnaise sauce. In my mind's eye I can see the table in the sunshine on the boulevard where this dish was served!

The value of the cabbage, from the point of view of its vitamin content, mineral content, and so on, is sometimes three or four times as high when eaten raw as when cooked. There is no doubt that the health of the nation as a whole will improve when more and more salads are eaten and less and less cooking is done. Children, who often find boiled cabbage uninteresting, and so consistently aim to leave it out of their diet, will almost literally dive into the salad bowl in order to make certain that they get their fair share. Grated cabbage served in this way they find nutty, palatable and attractive.

Hints on Preparation

Though it is true to say that cabbages eaten raw are more digestible than those cooked, it is equally true to insist that before serving, the leaves should always be grated or minced, the really coarse stalks being taken out and put on the compost heap. The bigger outside leaves are, perhaps, not as delicious as the centre of the hearts. Grated cabbage may either be served alone or be mixed with grated root vegetables and a little minced onion. The grated golden heart of a cabbage looks most attractive when served in small heaps in cup-like lettuce leaves. A horse-radish sauce is delicious served with grated cabbage, especially if the whole is garnished with some finely chopped parsley and a little paprika.

Later on will be found instructions as well as special hints and tips in respect of the individual members of the ' cabbage family ' and these naturally appear under their appropriate headings. The main principle, however, which must be emphasised in respect of all members of this family, is that they should be cut fresh, grated fresh, and served fresh.

THE BORECOLE OR KALE

The very name, Borecole, gives the clue to its popularity, for it is a Dutch word meaning the peasants' cabbage. It is a crop which grows well in a small garden and fortunately succeeds in quite a poor soil. It is hardy, requires very little attention and does not let the gardener down even in the frostiest weather. There are many kinds of kales, most of which are delicious when used in mixed salads.

All the kales come in at a time when other salads are scarce, that is to say, in the depth of winter and in the very early spring. They are the kind of plant that you can cut and come again, for they keep growing. I always cut the shoots when they are young so as to ensure the tenderest of salads and this does give the plants the chance of growing out again and producing a second crop and even a third crop. Don't make the mistake, however, of denuding the plants of leaves, just cut off one or two at a time and thus the supply will continue. If you overcut at any particular period the plants will suffer badly.

It has been stated that the Curly Kale is richer in carbohydrates, protein and salts than any other member of the cabbage family. It is also rich in vitamins A and C and can, therefore, take the place of the orange or blackcurrant juice in a child's diet.

There are variegated kales which look extremely attractive in the salad bowl because of their colours; there is the variegated silver, for instance, and the variegated purple. There is the Asparagus kale which produces long shoots of delicious flavour, the Green Curled Scotch Kale which is handsome and closely curled, the Tall Green Curled is said by some epicures to make the best salad, while the Russian Kale has that different flavour which some people have described as ' spinachy ' and others as ' nutty '.

The Soil

As has already been suggested, almost any soil will do for kale. They are excellent as a follow-on crop, for they can be planted immediately after harvesting the early potatoes or after early peas, French beans, spinach or lettuce. There should be no need to carry out any special manuring, for the plant foods and humus left behind by the previous crop should do. Just fork the ground over thoroughly and add an organic fertiliser like a fish manure at 4 ounces to the square yard. Carbonate of lime should be given as a top dressing at 5 ounces to the square yard, unless the crop recently harvested was given lime.

Sowing the Seed

As you probably will only want a few plants, you can choose a little bed, say, 3 feet by 3 feet, in which the various members of the cabbage family could be sown 6 inches apart. The beds should be in a sunny position and the surface of the soil should be raked down fine. There may be a certain amount of treading to do, as advised in Chapter II, so as to make certain that the bed is not puffy. The seed will be sown thinly in drills half-an-inch deep and when the plants come through and are large enough to handle, they should be thinned out to 6 inches apart.

The thinnings, if desired, may be transplanted to another bed on the 6 inch square basis. As a rule, however, if the sowing is thinly done, one can allow the plants to remain in the rows fairly close together until they are put out into their permanent quarters.

Most of the kale should be sown about the third or fourth week of April, but the Asparagus kale is not usually sown until mid-June or the end of June. Don't sow any earlier in either case, because when that is done the plants tend to go to seed in the spring.

Planting Out

Do the planting if possible at the beginning of July, the dwarfer being planted 2 feet square and the taller kinds 3 feet square. Don't attempt to plant closer for poor results will only occur. If the weather is dry, put water into the holes at planting time for it is important to see that the kales get away to a good start. Take precautions against the Club Root disease if necessary.

Cultivation

There is nothing to be done after planting, other than to keep the ground hoed.

Harvesting

Never cut the plants until early in the New Year unless it is absolutely necessary; the whole idea is to allow them to build up large, strong specimens before they are cut. Take some of the side shoots first because it is important to allow the head to encourage the production of more side shoots and to give them some protection. Last of all, remove the head prior to pulling up the plants.

BROCCOLI

It must be remembered that the modern broccoli is really a winter type of cauliflower. It is claimed by some that the curds are not so pure in texture as the cauliflower but it is difficult, owing to 'inter-marriages', to distinguish between the two. By careful sowings and correct planting it is possible to produce beautiful white curds every week from the Michaelmas day of one year to the middle of June of the next. I wouldn't advise readers in the north to grow this crop nor is it worth while concentrating on it in a small garden. Broccoli, however, grows very well indeed in the south and south-west.

The white curds of the broccoli are delicious in salads. It is possible, for instance, to mix grated raw cauliflower with grated radish and serve with mustard and cress or finely chopped parsley. Some people prefer the grated raw cauliflower mixed with the pulp of tomatoes and served in crisp, cup-like lettuce leaves, covered with a special home-made salad dressing, or mayonnaise and garnished with parsley. The curd of the cauliflower can be mixed with any salad and gives that particularly exciting flavour which can be obtained from no other vegetable.

The curds of broccoli may also be used for hors d'œuvres mixed with chopped onion and finely grated carrot. There is no doubt that the keen and ingenious reader will find numerous ways of using pieces of curd of broccoli cut up into various sizes for embellishing salads or for serving with hors d'œuvres of all kinds.

The Soil

The main requirement in the broccoli is to have firm soil and so it is a good plan not to dig in any well rotted compost just before planting. When this is done, soft growth is encouraged and the plants then tend to succumb to the winter. On the other hand, of course, it is best to use land that was well manured for the previous crop for it is useless to try and grow broccoli on poor soil. The gardener says that the ground should be 'in good heart'; that means that it is rich in humus but has not necessarily been freshly manured. When forking the ground over, however, a complete organic fertiliser, like a fish manure, with a 6 per cent potash content may be used at 4 ounces to the square yard.

Sowing the Seed

The seed bed should be prepared as advised for Borecole. Tiny drills, half-an-inch deep should be got out with a draw hoe, 9 inches apart, as soon as the tilth is really fine and the bed firm. In some gardens birds are fond of the seedlings when they come through, and to protect them, black cotton should be strung from short pieces of bamboo about 1 foot above soil level. Black cotton is always better than white cotton. Sow the seed of the earlier varieties about the middle of April and the seed of the late kinds about the middle of May. Thin out the seedlings if necessary to about 4 inches apart in the seed bed, for you should never allow the seedlings to become long and lanky. Protect against flea beetles by dusting the seedlings the moment they come through with Derris Dust and if the garden is subject to Club Root take the necessary precautions as stated in a leaflet which the author will send gratis to any reader of this book who encloses a stamped addressed envelope.

Planting Out

Do the planting out as soon as the land is ready and when the plants are about 6 inches high. I always plant them after French beans, early peas or early potatoes and thus no ground is wasted. Put plenty of water into the holes at planting time if the weather is dry and see that they are really firm in the soil. Normally the planting should be done 2 feet by 2 feet, though with the larger and later varieties I usually plant 3 feet by 3 feet.

Cultivation

Hoe regularly to keep down weeds and about the beginning of November, if the garden is rather exposed, take a little soil out with a trowel to the North of the plants and with the heel push the plants over so that they incline somewhat in this direction. Then put the soil that you have taken out with the trowel, on the other side and press it down well with the idea of keeping the plants in an inclined position. If the plants seem to flag after the heeling over process, water them well for two or three days.

Harvesting

Cut the white curds immediately they are ready, but if it happens that several curds turn in at a time, break a leaf or two over the plants that are not immediately required with the idea of keeping them back. As a last resort, if too many are ready at any particular moment, pull the plants up, root and all, and hang them upside down in a shed. There the curds will keep for some time without spoiling.

Types

For the autumn there is Veitch's Self-Protecting, or for those who live in the south-west, Extra Early Roscoff. For the winter: there is for late December and early January, New Year; for mid-January and early February, Early Feltham or, for those who live in the south and south-west, Early Roscoff No. 2. For March, there is Mid-Feltham; for April, Snow's Winter White; for May, Late Feltham, and for June, Clucas's June. For those who live in the south and south-west, more Roscoff's can be grown for this period, i.e., Roscoff No. 3 and Roscoff No. 4.

BROCCOLI SPROUTING

No good gardener would think of being without this ideal winter crop. Instead of growing the normal large white curd, it produces a number of delicious elongated flowering heads as shown in the drawing. It is very hardy indeed and goes on producing the desired shoots for several months, while at the end of the season the leaves can be eaten also. There are two main types – the Purple Sprouting and the Green Sprouting, sometimes called White Sprouting. The Calabresse, or Italian Sprouting Broccoli is the earliest and must be kept cut as the heads are produced, or else it ceases to crop satisfactorily.

The Soil

Exactly the same type of soil is needed as described under the heading ' Borecole '.

Sowing the Seed

Sow the seeds of most of the types as advised for Broccoli in April and then the crop will be ready for use the following Spring. Sow the Italian Sprouting Broccoli at the same time; this will be used in September and October.

Planting out

The moment the plants are about 6 inches high and the land is ready, set the plants out 2 feet square. Plant firmly and water-in if the soil is dry. I often sow a row of radish or spinach in between the rows as an inter-crop or catch-crop and thus no room is wasted.

Cultivation

Hoe lightly but regularly in between the rows until a hard winter makes this unnecessary.

Cutting the Sprouting Broccoli.

Harvesting

Do not attempt to do any cutting until the flower shoots are found to be growing out in between the axils of the leaves. When these shoots are about 6 inches long they should be cut to within an inch of their base, then more of the shoots will be produced. It is when they are soft and tender that they can be cut up for serving in salads. These will be cut up in their turn. Finally, when all the plants have finished sprouting, the leaves will be eaten. Lastly, the stalks will be pulled up. They will be well bashed up with the back of an axe on a chopping block and will go on the compost heap.

Types

The earliest type is the Italian, but this is soon followed by the Christmas Extra Early Purple. Next comes the Early Sprouting Purple for late February and early March and finally the Late Sprouting Purple which is usually cut in April.

BRUSSELS SPROUTS

This is regarded by some as a very common green vegetable. Actually, if the correct varieties are grown and the picking is done at the right time, the sprouts are delicious in a salad. They must, however, be gathered when they are young and tender, that is to say when they are no larger than half-an-inch across. To use them in salads they should be grated or put through the mincer. Some people prefer to separate the little leaves of individual sprouts before putting them in a salad, but this takes a lot of time. Sprouts are very rich in salts, carbohydrates and proteins and they stand next to Borecole in nutritive value, containing as they do vitamins A and C.

A delicious salad consists of chopped Brussels sprouts and grated cheese. The author has used this with success as a filling for sandwiches made with wholemeal bread or when put into mounds on digestive biscuits. It is important never to use any of the yellowing outside leaves of the sprout in a salad; it is equally important to start harvesting the sprouts from the base of the plants upwards. Do this harvesting with a sharp knife, leaving a tiny piece of stem from the base of the sprout on the main stem of the plant. This will ensure that you will get a secondary crop of baby sprouts, even if they tend to be loose and open. Once all the sprouts have been picked then the centre of the head of each sprout plant will come into use for the salad bowl also.

The Soil

The Brussels Sprout prefers heavy land because it likes firm soil. The roots of the plant go down deeply and for this reason expert sprout growers leave the land alone and so plant in firm natural soil. If the land is inclined to be poor, plenty of well-rotted compost should be used as a mulch on the soil. The author uses one good barrow load to 4 square yards and applies the organic matter on the top of the land 2 inches deep.

Prior to planting out the sprouts, a complete organic fertiliser, like a fish manure, is given at 4 ounces to the square yard, this being lightly hoed in. Two months after planting, old soot is applied along the rows at the rate of a handful to the yard wide.

Sowing the Seed

Those who like very early Brussels Sprouts must sow the seeds early in September of the one year in order to have good plants to put out in the May of the next year. Here they live through the winter until the ground is ready where they are to crop. Seeds can be sown in frames or under cloches in January or February – this is done because the Brussels Sprout prefers a long season of growth. Those who have no frames or cloches may sow out of doors early in March. It is true that some people sow as late as early April, but this isn't really fair on this tall growing, heavy cropping vegetable.

Transplanting, of course, can always be done when the seedlings are fit to be moved; the largest plants should be got out at the first transplanting, but the original bed should be gone over again a fortnight later, and the largest plants removed for transplanting once more. This procedure may be followed yet a third time. It is in this way that successive batches can be obtained for planting out in the open, with the result that there will be successive and continuous pickings over a long period.

Of course, the usual precautions must be taken against the Club Root disease, the Cabbage Root Maggot and the Flea Beetle. Further, lime should always be given as a surface dressing prior to planting out, at say, 6 ounces to the square yard. This latter dressing may only be omitted when the ground is known to be very limey.

Planting Out

Not only do Brussels Sprouts need a long season of growth if they are to crop heavily but, in addition, they look for plenty of room for development. Plant therefore in May or early June on the 3 feet square basis, though if the garden is small and the ground known to be poor, $2\frac{1}{2}$ feet square will do. I often take an inter-crop of French beans in between the rows or sow summer lettuce or spinach.

Cultivation

Hoe carefully throughout the summer and make certain not to injure the leaves or the stems. Remember, it is the big leaves on the sprout plants that provide the food to produce the sprouts themselves and they should, therefore, never be cut off until they start to turn yellow and so are useless. The head of the plants must be kept on for the same reason until the end of February. Keep a sharp look-out the whole time for the Blue Aphis, often called the Blue Bug, and the White Fly. Spray the plants well with Liquid Derris or with a pyrethrum wash, or with the two mixed together, if any of these pests are seen.

Harvesting

As has already been said, the sprouts should be cut and not just broken. Further, this should always be done systematically, starting at the bottom of each plant. Don't, whatever you do, cut all the sprouts from one plant and leave the next one. Take the trouble to go over all the plants, cutting the sprouts that are needed from each one.

Types

There is Peer Gynt, an Early which produces sprouts of good quality, King Arthur, a Main Crop, and Cambridge No. 5, a Late Variety which I consider produces the best sprouts for eating raw.

CABBAGE

The cabbage is, of course, the most common member of this family, but has the great advantage of being available all the year round. Sowings of various types and varieties can be made in March, April, May and July. Of all the types, those known as the spring cabbages are perhaps the most to be desired, being particularly delicious in salads at a time when lettuces are scarce, i.e. April and early May. The white-hearted winter cabbages are also very popular and rightly so.

Eaten raw, the cabbage is ideal, containing as it does vitamins A, B and C, and being particularly digestible. The white hearts, though they may look more appetising, are not so rich in minerals as the green hearts. Before using cabbages, take out the coarse stalks and then mince or grate.

Always take the utmost care against Club Root Disease, the Cabbage Root Maggot and Flea Beetle.

Planting Out

Plant out the July sowings in mid-September. Plant out the April sowings mid-June. Plant out the May sowings late in July.

The distances apart should be: for the July sowings, 18 inches by 18 inches; for the April sowings, 2 feet by 18 inches; and for the early May sowings, 2 feet by 2 feet.

Cultivation

Hoe regularly between the plants and if possible give copious waterings in dry weather. It is no good giving sprinklings; flooding must be done.

Harvesting

Cut regularly, as the firm hearts are ready, and if too many heads should be ready to cut together, pull the plants up with their root attached and hang them upside down in a shed.

Types

For planting in the autumn, Unwins Foremost; for sowing in April, Autumn Pride; for sowing earlier in the spring, Primo; and for sowing mid-April, Winter Keeper, which turns in for use in November.

RED CABBAGE

The red cabbage makes an excellent pickle. The cabbage should be shredded thinly on to a large dish, sprinkled with salt and left for 24 hours, after which the liquid should be drained off. Meantime, sufficient spiced vinegar should be prepared to cover the cabbage. To do this, put the vinegar into a pan with a little crushed root ginger and allspice ($\frac{1}{2}$ ounce of each to each quart of vinegar will do) and boil the whole up together. The cabbage should then be packed into bottles and the vinegar poured over whilst still hot, but the bottle should not be sealed till the vinegar is quite cold.

Red cabbage can also be shredded up raw, placed in a bowl, covered with a cupful of vinegar and 2 tablespoonfuls of salad oil and sprinkled with a tablespoonful of salt and a teaspoonful of pepper. After mixing, allow to stand for 2 days before serving. The cabbage is thus softened and much of the dressing is absorbed.

Sowing the Seed

It should be sown in exactly the same way as described for cabbage. The seed may either be sown in March or April, or often in August in the north, and as the result of autumn sowing, the heads are fit to cut the following autumn.

Types

Particularly good types are Ruby Ball, one of the earliest; and Danish Stonehead, which is of a particularly deep red colour.

SAVOYS

Savoys have got a bad name, in some areas, because farmers have grown the giant kinds suitable for feeding cows, and these were sold for human consumption in the shops! Good varieties – if they are well grown – are delicious to eat raw after the first frosts. The outside leaves should be dispensed with, being fed to rabbits for meat production, or poultry for egg production, and the hearts should be cut up fine. Being hardy and delicately flavoured, they do fulfil a need.

Sowing the Seed.

The Savoy can be sown in exactly the same way as the cabbage, the important difference being, that it likes firm ground. Normally the seed is sown in three batches, the first in the middle of March, the second early in April, and the third at the end of April.

These sowings produce plants that are put out at the end of June, the middle of July and the end of July. The rows should be 18 inches apart and the plants 15 inches in the rows.

Types
 Delicious types to use raw are: Drumhead, Ormskirk Early for October, Omega for November, December and January; and Ormskirk Late for February and March.

CHAPTER VIII

PEAS AND BEANS AS SALADS

Most people like peas raw, and it is seldom that you can take a boy or girl down a row without their pulling a pod or two and eating the delicious sweet young peas therein. There is no reason at all, therefore, why all the peas you have grown shouldn't be eaten raw if desired and the more the pods are picked when young, the heavier the crop will be.

Whilst peas make a tasty salad on their own, they are particularly good when mixed with other salad plants. Sugar peas and Asparagus peas are doubly useful, for if picked when young both pods and peas can be eaten. Successive sowings of peas can, of course, keep up the supply over very long periods. It is possible, for instance, to pick the first pods in June, as the result of growing under cloches, and to continue picking right throughout the season.

Broad beans, too, are delicious eaten raw with salt, providing they are gathered when young. Few people pick broad beans early enough and because of this are disappointed that the centre of the beans are somewhat on the tough side. Small French beans also can be cut up and used in salads and it is surprising how tender and delicious they are.

The great advantage of broad beans is that they are richer in protein than any other vegetable grown in Great Britain and are almost as rich as the parsnip when eaten raw. They also contain the vitamins A, B and C and are better eaten in a salad that does not contain any other starchy food such as potato. It is when broad beans are eaten with a meat dish that so many people find them indigestible.

BROAD BEANS

Eaten raw the broad bean is delicious – though because the beans are eaten young some people think they are wasteful! If however, you love raw young broad beans as I do, then you will certainly have 2 or 3 rows in the average garden, so as to provide variety of food. A great advantage of the broad bean is that the stalk, or straw as it is called, is so useful when dried, and may be used to form mats to give protection to frames or to act as a wind break. The 'straw' when burnt is also very rich in potash and may be used, therefore, as a fertiliser. The roots, too, of the broad beans add nitrogen to the ground if they are left in the soil at harvesting.

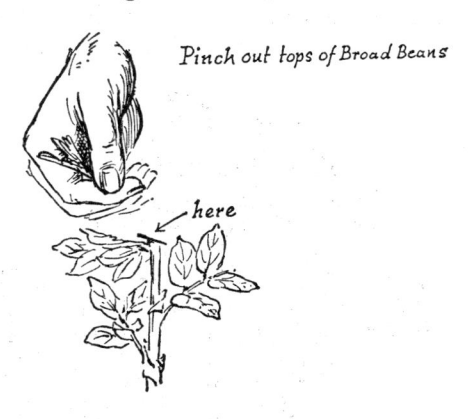

Pinch out tops of Broad Beans

here

The Soil

Almost any soil will do and the only preparation necessary will be the forking in lightly of the composted vegetable refuse at one good barrow load to 8 square yards. In addition, fish manure should be added at 3 ounces to the square yard and wood ashes to 5 ounces per square yard.

Sedge peat, by the way, can always be used instead of compost, where it is not available.

Sowing the Seed

The seed should be sown at two periods:
 1. November and January, the Long Pod types.
 2. March and April, the Windsor types.

The November and January sowings are not always successful unless they are covered by continuous cloches. The rows should be 2 feet 6 inches apart. Drills should be drawn out 5 inches wide with a draw hoe, and 3 to 4 inches deep. The beans should be spaced out in these drills, zig-zag fashion, 6 inches apart. It is advisable to sow a dozen beans at the end of each row and the plants that result may be used for filling up any gaps that appear later.

Cultivation

Use the hoe regularly, and keep down the Black Fly. This may be done by spraying with Liquid Derris directly it appears. The tops may be pinched out when the bottom beans are forming to encourage early production, but this isn't really necessary.

Pick broad beans while still only about four inches long

Broad beans.

Harvesting

Pick regularly, when the pods are, say, 4 inches long. They are then delicious.

Types

Dwarf Bush for a very dwarf early variety, followed by Exhibition White Windsor. Longfellow is perhaps the tallest growing Long Pod type and bears enormous pods. Red Epicure is another particularly delicious variety.

FRENCH BEANS

The French Bean is given various names including the Dwarf Bean and Kidney Bean. It withstands dry conditions better than any other crop. As mentioned in the introduction to this chapter, the French bean to be eaten raw *must* be picked when young and tender. It will soon be possible to find, by experiment, the optimum size. Syringing the plants over with clean water every day helps to keep the pods fresh and enables them to be eaten raw a little larger than normally. Mulching the rows with sedge peat an inch deep also helps greatly in ensuring that the beans remain fresh and succulent longer.

Cut the beans up after they have been pulled and serve them, either alone as a salad, or mixed with lettuce, endive and the other salad plants. They make a very good salad with sliced tomato to which a little chopped onion has been added.

The Soil

If the french beans prefer one soil to another it is the light land, and to get the best results, plenty of well composted organic matter should be forked in to a depth of 2 inches or so, beforehand. Land that is rich in humus produces the most tender beans. It is usual to crop the land with lettuces first of all, in such a way that the french beans can be sown actually in between the rows. The lettuces give protection to the bean plants when they are coming through, and by the time they need the room the lettuces should be harvested and used.

Lime is certainly necessary and should be applied to the surface of the ground; carbonate of lime, for instance, at about 5 to 6 ounces per square yard. This may be omitted in the case of chalky soils known to be rich in lime.

Sowing the Seed

There are four main sowing times:
1. Sow in March in frames and grow on in frames.
2. Sow early in April in frames and plant outside.
3. Sow outside in May.
4. Sow outside early in July.

In the case of (1) the plants should stand 9 inches square and may either be transplanted into further frames or sown at this distance apart in the original frames. In the case of (2) the plants are put outside in a sheltered border the second week of May, care being taken to see that there is plenty of soil attached to the roots.

For the outside sowings, the drills should be 4 inches wide and 2 inches deep, conveniently made with a draw hoe. They should be from 2 to 3 feet apart, depending on the height of the variety. The beans should be sown zig-zag fashion, 6 inches apart in these drills. Twelve beans should be sown in a ring at the end of each row, the plants that result being put out into the rows where gaps appear.

The July sowing is usually done with the rows 2 feet apart, the beans being spaced out to 10 inches apart, in a narrow drill, 3 inches deep.

Cultivation

Hoe regularly, drawing the soil up to the plants, rather than away from them. If the plants grow tall, give them some bushy, twiggy sticks as support.

Harvesting

Pick regularly when young and this will help to ensure the maximum crop.

Types

The Wonder is a good variety for sowing in frames or under cloches. Black Wonder is first-rate because it is resistant to a disease called Halo Blight. Bounteous can usually be eaten raw larger than other types and Feltham Prolific is a dwarf variety that can be planted closer in the rows than any others.

PEAS

Peas, like broad beans, enrich the soil if the roots are left in the ground. The great thing when eating peas raw is to pick them, if possible, just before eating. If they are gathered the day before they tend to harden. Pick, therefore, as required and shell as late as possible before a meal. If they have to be shelled some time beforehand, they should be wrapped in a damp cloth and left in a cool place.

As is suggested at the beginning of the chapter, peas on the whole are best used as an addition to other forms of salad, though those who are really fond of them, like Louis XIV of France, may like to eat them alone even without any salad dressing at all. Sprinkled with salt, fresh young peas have proved a good hors d'œuvre dish. Cucumbers and peas make a good salad, especially if the former are cut up into dice about 1 inch square.

The Soil
If the land is properly limed most soils will grow peas well. They do dislike acid ground, however. The quantity of lime to be used may easily be gauged by using a B.D.H. Soil Indicator which can be obtained from any reliable chemist for a reasonable sum. The ground to be used should be forked over lightly about 2 to 3 inches deep, well-composted organic matter being incorporated at the rate of one barrowload to 4 square yards. In addition, use a complete organic fertiliser like a fish manure at 3 to 4 ounces to the square yard. Directly the plants are through some dried blood may be sprinkled along the rows at 2 ounces per yard run so as to encourage growth and hurry the plants along. Top dressings of sedge peat, put along the rows of the plants act as a mulch and so help to retain the moisture, and in addition, of course, they add essential organic matter to the ground. The secret is not to put them on deeper than 1 inch.

Sowing the Seed
With a draw hoe, draw out drills 5 to 6 inches wide and 3 inches deep. Sow the peas about 2 inches apart in these drills, scattered evenly. Later varieties may be sown 3 inches apart. To secure immediate germination, soak the peas overnight in cold water, or if it is feared that birds or mice will make depredations, soak for two or three hours in a mixture of paraffin and red lead made up to the consistency of Devonshire cream.

Protect the plants from damage by birds, as they come

D*

through, by using home-made or bought pea guards, or by covering with continuous cloches. Dust with Derris Dust if the pea and bean weevils are nibbling semi-circular holes out of the leaves.

There are five main sowing periods:
1. Sow November or December under continuous cloches or under Dutch lights.
2. Sow January or early February in boxes or pots in the greenhouse or frames.
3. Sow February (south) or March (north) out of doors.
4. Sow outside at the beginning of April.
5. Sow late June or the beginning of July to pick in September or early October.

The peas sown in pots or boxes have to be planted out in the open in rows late in March or early in April. From the beginning of April onwards, where there is room, it is a good plan to make another sowing immediately the previous row is seen above the ground. As to distances apart between the rows, this of course, depends on the varieties; 4-foot high varieties need 2 feet of space on either side of them, while 3-foot high varieties only need 18 inches space between the rows, and so on.

Cultivation

Regular hoeing to keep down weeds between the rows. A certain amount of hand weeding in the rows, if necessary. Good floodings from time to time in small drills drawn out on either side of the rows, rather than on the rows themselves.

Twiggy branches should always be used, up which the peas can climb, except in the case of the very dwarf varieties which only grow 18 inches high or so. Put the sticks in at an angle of 45 degrees so that the row on one side of the peas slopes one way, and the row on the other side slopes the other way. Give mulchings of grass mowings along the rows when the weather is dry, but never deeper than 1 inch.

Harvesting

Regular picking is a vital necessity, for if only one pod is left on to get old – the plant suffers. Be careful, therefore, not to miss any when picking.

Types

There are many different varieties to choose from and it is very difficult to make a satisfactory choice. Suggestions are: Histon Mini, 12 inches; Forward, a first early, 2 feet; Recette, an early, 2 feet; Onward, which is mildew-resisting, $2\frac{1}{2}$ feet; and Lord Chancellor, a first-class marrowfat, 5 feet, for a late.

CHAPTER IX

ROOT CROPS AS SALADS

UNFORTUNATELY there are not a very large number of root crops which can be eaten raw. It is true that under famine conditions most roots have been eaten in a raw condition and have supported life in consequence, but the majority of them are not particularly appetising uncooked. The beetroot, for instance, tastes a little earthy, though many like it when mixed with other roots; the parsnip is rather hard, though even this root can be eaten raw when young and is on the sweet side. These latter remarks also apply to the salsify and scorzonera.

Roots will, however, keep and most of them are rich in vitamins A, B_1, B_2 and B_3. All of them may be 'forced', that is to say, that once they have been harvested in the autumn, they can be stood in a dark warm place where they will send out numerous fresh tender yellowy shoots. These can be used as salads, and in the winter time when there is little else, the tops of the forced swede or forced large carrot come in very useful indeed.

Some of the roots, like the turnip, swede or Spanish radish, give that 'hot' flavour to a salad which so many people like, and so are useful in cold weather. To get the best results from them it is necessary to wash them well with plenty of clean water and to see that they are scrubbed really clean. If the outside skins are tough these may be peeled off, the peelings being use to feed rabbits and chickens, or even to be thrown on the vegetable compost heap to rot down for manure. The roots should then be grated or passed through a mincing machine. It is when they are in a fine condition that they are more digestible, more attractive, and are more easily mixed into a salad. Finely grated carrot – because of its reddish colour – adds a distinctive note to the salad bowl.

BEETROOT

The Soil

On the whole beetroot prefer a lightish soil. They tend to be somewhat coarse on heavy land. Heavy clay should be made lighter, therefore, by forking in plenty of sand, burnt earth, flue dust or similar 'lightening' material – you'll need a great deal! Sedge peat can also be used to improve heavy soils. Apply it at 2 bucketfuls to the square yard. When soils are shallow and stony, it is better to grow the Globe varieties than the long types. Those who live at the seaside should always use well-rotted seaweed as a manure, at the rate of one barrowload to 10 square yards. (Fresh farmyard manure or dung should not be used.)

In addition to seaweed, hop manure, finely divided wool shoddy, or sedge peat may be forked into the top 4 or 5 inches at 1 bucketful to the square yard. Wood ashes are useful in addition, if applied at 6 ounces to the square yard while, generally speaking, a fish manure will do all that is needed, if applied at 4 ounces to the square yard.

Where these large, long beets are to be grown, deep cultivation is necessary and they are useful, therefore, to follow such crops as celery and leeks. Few people, however, bother about them today.

Sowing the Seed

The seed should be sown either at the end of April or the beginning of May, though in the south one or two rows may be put in at the end of March. Normally the drills should be 2 inches deep and 15 inches apart, but at the March sowing, the drills may be as close as 1 foot. Gardeners in the north often delay to the 15th May because of late frosts. A summer sowing may be made in July, in addition, so as to obtain fresh young roots in the autumn and winter.

Cultivation

Though it is wise to sow the seed very thinly, even then it will probably be necessary to thin the plants out, first of all to

4 inches apart, and then when the roots are the size of golf balls, to 8 inches apart. The roots at this second thinning may be eaten and are delicious. The young leaves of these thinnings, too, are very tender and should be shredded up and put into a mixed salad. You can, of course, do 'station' sowing as explained in Chapter II.

It is sometimes necessary to protect the young seedlings when they first come through, with black cotton strung on short sticks, or fish netting, because birds are very partial to them. Those who use cloches find these ideal, because they not only hurry the beetroot along, but protect the seedlings from birds also.

Hoe regularly between the rows to keep down the weeds and do a certain amount of hand weeding in the rows to ensure that the plants have the best chance. If the weather is dry, sprinkle a little salt along the rows and hoe this in, for it will help to 'attract' and hold the moisture. Be careful not to touch the roots with the hoe or they will bleed, and don't use salt, by the way, if the soil is heavy clay – because it may ruin the texture of the land.

Harvesting

Either pull the roots as they are required, or leave them in the ground until they are required in the winter. To make certain that the pulling can be done at any time during frosty periods, cover the rows with straw or bracken or cloches. Generally speaking, however, it is better to pull the roots up in the autumn or early winter and store them in heaps in the open, covered first of all with straw and then with plenty of soil in the same way as potatoes are treated. These heaps are known as 'buries', 'hogs' or 'clamps' and when it is impossible to store the roots under cover, this method of storage proves very useful out of doors. Cut the tops off before storing, but be care-

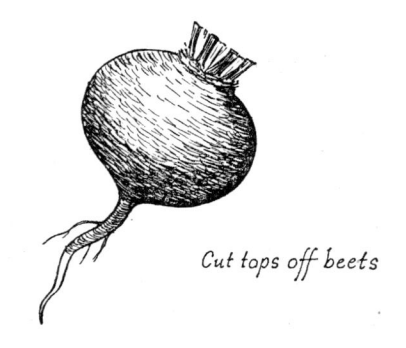

Cut tops off beets

ful not to do this too near the crown or bleeding may take place. Properly clamped, or kept in sand or dry earth in a frost-proof shed or store, the roots will keep quite easily until the following June.

Varieties

Two very good Globe types are Early Wonder (really early) and Boltardy which is a nice round beet, free from white rings inside. A delicious Intermediate type is known at Spangsjberg Cylinder – this is what is called tankard-shaped.

Preparation

When beetroot is grated raw – really finely – it goes well in a mixed salad and is a useful addition to the colour effect. It is always better to grate as short a time as possible before the beetroot is to be used – or it turns black and sometimes slimy! Cooked beetroot can be cut into squares and used in a mixed salad or can be sliced and served with salad dressing or vinegar.

CARROTS

Fortunately carrots can be sown, sown and sown again, and by successive sowings it is possible to get fresh young roots during the whole of the summer and autumn. There is no difficulty in producing them during the winter in warm borders and in frames, if necessary, while very early results can be achieved under cloches.

Raw carrots are rich in vitamins A and C and in many of the needful salts. When grated they are very juicy and particularly digestible, but, as in the case of beetroot, they must be freshly grated, for if they are cut up or minced and left in the air for an hour or more, they harden, lose their colour and cease to be attractive. If they have to be grated some time beforehand, they should be kept in a damp cloth and covered with a plate to exclude the air. The carrots will keep well in a plastic or polythene bag placed in a jug.

Many like grated carrots alone, but the author prefers them mixed with chopped sprouts, grated cabbage and turnips. If chives, parsley and a few fresh peas can be added, so much the better. Grated carrot and raw onion are very good mixed together, as are grated carrots and celery. There is no need to stick to the young carrots, the older, more bolder roots being particularly delicious, especially when what are called the coreless varieties are grown.

Naturally the Shorthorns and Early types should be grown on the shallower soils. The Intermediates may be grown on the deeper soils and the really Long types are usually grown as main crops on deep loams. Where soils are fairly shallow, the Intermediates have to be grown as the maincrops.

The Soil

The best results will be achieved on a deep, well-cultivated sandy loam; the very sandy soils will be improved by working in shallowly plenty of finely divided organic matter such as damped sedge peat. Really heavy clays should be opened up by working into the ground sandy or gritty material such as sand, flue dust, or burnt soil. Even here, sedge peat will help tremendously, if used at 2 bucketfuls to the square yard. It is on the heavier soils that the shorter types should be grown.

In all cases it is necessary to get the surface of the soil down to a fine condition before attempting to sow the seed. A good fish manure may be added during preparation at 4 to 5 ounces to the square yard, and in addition, early carrots may always be hurried along if a little nitrogen, in the form of dried blood, is sprinkled along the rows at 1 ounce to the square yard run. There should be a fortnight or three weeks between each application.

Sowing the Seed

The earliest sowing out of doors can be made in a sunny situation during the months of February or March, the drills being 9 inches apart. In the north, protection will have to be given to such sowings with cloches, while if cloches are used in the south, sowing may be carried out as early as late January. Normal maincrop sowing will be made in April in drills 12 inches apart, though with the large maincrop varieties, the rows need to be as far apart as 18 inches.

A further sowing may be made in May and yet another in

June, and the last sowing of an early variety will be done in the month of July, so that fresh young roots may be pulled in September and early October. This last sowing is often a broadcasting, instead of in drills in the normal manner.

To ensure thin sowing by whatever method adopted, it is advisable to mix the seed with two or three times its bulk of dry earth or sand. When really thin sowings are done in this way, there is no need for thinning later on, and thus there is much less risk of a bad attack of carrot fly.

Cultivation

Aim at thinning the main crop sowings to about 8 inches apart, and the thinnings pulled out of the ground for this purpose are usually large enough to use in salads, both tops and roots, for the thin sowing allows the roots to develop properly. The early varieties do not not have to be thinned when the seed is mixed with sand.

A Naphthalene dust should be applied *in between* the rows a week before thinning and a week afterwards, at 1 ounce to the yard run, in order to keep away the *carrot flies that cause the maggots in the roots. Hoe regularly along the rows to keep the ground weed free and the top ½ inch of soil loose. In dry weather it may be necessary, in addition, to ensure good germination, to give the rows a thorough flooding with water.

Harvesting

Pull the roots of the early varieties as and when they are required and use them while they are quite fresh. Lift the roots of the maincrops just before the frosty winter weather sets in. Cut off the tops and store in a bury or clamp as advised for beetroot. The roots will keep well under cover in a dry, frost-proof shed or cellar if there is some dry sand or soil mixed amongst them. It is usual to cover them with straw, dry sand or earth also.

Varieties

For the hotbed, heated frame, or greenhouse, Sweetheart;

---

* Sowing onion and carrots in alternate rows has been found to be effective in keeping both the carrot and onion flies away.

for the cold frame, Amsterdam Forcing; for the early border, Early Nantes; as a good maincrop, or where a long variety is required, sow James' Scarlet Intermediate.

RADISH

Whole books have been written about radishes, for they were one of the earliest grown vegetables and are undoubtedly one of the most popular salad plants. It is known that they were used in the days of the Pyramids and probably the educated Chinese used them long before this. They are easy to grow; they

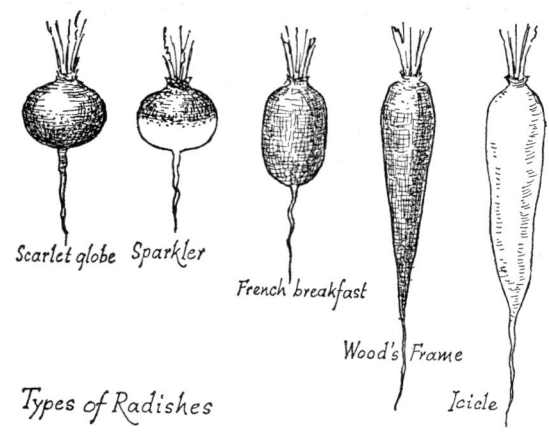

Scarlet globe   Sparkler

French breakfast

Wood's Frame

Icicle

Types of Radishes

come to maturity from seed more quickly than any other salad crop, for indeed to be at their best they must be grown quickly.

They can either be served whole, the leaves being eaten as well as the roots, or they can be topped and tailed before being mixed into the salad bowl. There are kinds which are crimson, others which are half white and half red, while some varieties are pure white.

The Soil

Fork into the top 2 or 3 inches finely divided organic matter, such as sedge peat, fully composted well-rotted leaves or similar material, at the rate of one bucketful to the square yard. Then, by alternate raking and treading, get the surface of the soil down to a fine tilth. If the ground is very poor or on the heavy side, dig in at a spade's depth, composted vegetable refuse at the rate of one good barrowload to 12 square yards. Give the surface of the soil a dressing of carbonate of lime afterwards – at 5 to 6 ounces to the square yard.

Sowing the Seed

The seed may either be sown thinly broadcast or better still in rows 6 inches apart, the drills being ½ inch deep. Radishes can often be sown as a catch crop on any vacant land. The seed may be sown at the same time as another crop, for instance, parsley, for the radish seed germinates quickly and so marks the rows and makes it easier for hoeing. The little radish roots are then pulled early and this gives the parsley a chance to develop properly.

Gardeners often cover a winter radish bed with straw 3 inches deep and remove this when the plants are really growing well. Always make the soil firm after sowing as this ensures the crispest roots. In the ordinary way, sowings will be made once a fortnight or every three weeks from the beginning of March to the beginning of September. In a dry, warm summer the July and August sowings should be done in a shady place.

Harvesting

Pull the radishes early while the roots are still young, fresh, and crisp.

Varieties

A good crimson round is Scarlet Globe; a half white and half red is Sparkler 50/50; a delicious oval is French Breakfast; a scarlet globe is Cherry Belle; and a crisp white is Icicle. By the way, buying packets of mixed radish seed is quite a good idea.

RADISHES, WINTER

Unfortunately, winter radishes are not so widely known as summer kinds. The roots grow large and look more like turnips. They are, however, just as delicious in salads when grated and cut up finely. Their great advantage is that they are perfectly happy if left in the ground during the winter and are not damaged by frost. They may, therefore, be dug up and used as required.

Sowing the Seed

The seed should be sown in July in the north, or about the middle of August in the south, in a fine but firm seed bed; the drills should be drawn out 9 inches apart and $\frac{1}{2}$ inch deep and, if the weather is dry, these should be given a good soaking. When the plants are about 1 inch high they should be thinned out to 6 inches apart, the thinnings being transplanted to any gaps that appear necessary. After such transplanting, a really good watering will have to be done every day for a week to prevent the transplanted radishes from going to seed.

Varieties

There are only two varieties of winter radish – one the Black Spanish, and the other, the China Rose. Both have long and round types.

SWEDES

There is no reason to sow what are called garden varieties, for the farm types of swedes are equally valuable and particularly delicious. They are said to be the more tender when they have been 'touched' or given their full flavour by the frost. Their calorific value stands at 145 and this means that they are valuable in a salad for warming the body in the winter.

To serve swedes raw it is necessary first of all to wash the roots well and then peel off the rough outer skin. The inside flesh should then be grated or minced before being put into the salad bowl. Swedes go well with other minced root crops such as carrots, beetroot and radishes and make quite a delicious dish when mixed with grated raw onions. They can, of course, be used with lettuce, endive, forced dandelion or any similar green salad crop.

The Soil

Almost any soil is suitable for the swede. It is a crop that will grow even in the coldest parts because it is so hardy. Into poor land fork in lightly any finely divided organic matter such as advised for radishes, at say, one good barrowload to 9 square yards. A good fish manure should then be raked into the top 2 or 3 inches at 4 to 5 ounces to the square yard.

Swedes are subject to Club Root and necessary precautions should therefore be taken. The surface of the ground should be limed – carbonate of lime being used at the rate of 5 to 7 ounces to the square yard.

Sowing the Seed

Sow the seed in drills 18 inches apart and $\frac{1}{2}$ inch deep. It is better to space the seeds out in groups of three, say, 6 inches apart in the drills – for thinning will have to be done later when the plants are 2 to 3 inches high – to 1 foot apart. In the south it is usual to sow early in June and in the north in May.

Cultivation

Keep down the Turnip Flea Beetle by dusting regularly with a Derris – Pyrethrum dust. Be sure to buy this particular product, although it is often sold under proprietary names, because it is so effective. In very dry weather it is necessary to flood the ground, rather than water, to get the plants going.

Harvesting

The roots may be dug up as required. They can be left in the ground throughout the winter and, as has already been said, the roots are particularly delicious after they have been 'touched' by the frost.

Varieties

There are very many types of swedes from which to choose. Superlative is tankard-shaped; Kangaroo is very hardy; while Field Purple Top is said by epicures to have the best flavour.

TURNIPS

There are two main groups of turnips. First of all, the six-week types which are used when they are about the size of a tennis ball. These can be sown outside early or even late. Then there are the main winter turnips whose seed is put into the ground in July and August, the roots being pulled in the early winter. The large-sized Main Sowings are pulled in the late summer.

Turnips can be used raw in salads and give a similar flavour to radishes. The six-week types are very delicious for this purpose, especially if pulled on the young side while they are fresh and before the roots get coarse.

The Soil

The lighter sands should be enriched by having plenty of well-rotted and composted vegetable refuse forked in 2 or 3 inches deep. Into the top 2 inches should be raked a fertiliser with an organic base, like fish manure at 3 to 4 ounces to the square yard.

Sowing the Seed

The first seeds can be put into the open ground in the south, about mid-March in a fine sunny bed. Take every precaution against the Turnip Flea Beetle for all sowings, by dusting the seed first of all with Derris Pyrethrum dust and then, immediately the little plants are through, by dusting again with the same substance.

Draw out drills 1 foot apart and $\frac{1}{2}$ inch deep and having sown very thinly, rake the ground over afterwards to level and cover over the seeds. Even when every endeavour has been made to sow thinly, it is usually necessary to thin out, because turnips always do their best when no leaf of one root is allowed to touch a leaf of its neighbour. With the small varieties, thinning to 4 or 5 inches apart will be sufficient, but with the maincrop types a final thinning to 15 inches apart will be necessary. Curiously enough, the shortest plants always make the best roots, so when thinning always pull out the tallest and strongest specimens.

Cultivation

Hoe regularly between the rows and dust with Derris powder to keep away the Turnip Flea Beetles. In dry seasons, if water is available, give good floodings so as to ensure crisp tender roots.

Harvesting
Pull the spring and summer sown kinds as and when the roots are ready. Do not let them get too old or coarse.

Varieties
There is nothing better to grow in the access frame or under cloches than Tokyo Cross, and for early work outside, on a warm border, there is Early Snowball or Extra Early White Milan.
Two good maincrops are Golden Wonder and Golden Ball.

SALAD POTATOES

Purists may be shocked that I have included potatoes in the Chapter on Root crops. There is no chapter for Tuberous crops and so the salad potato does fit quite neatly in here.

Most people know how to grow ordinary potatoes, and when they have boiled them they cut them up and use them in salads. A well made potato salad is very popular and rightly so.

There are, however, special varieties of potatoes which the French and Italians use for salad purposes. There are one or two firms which stock these varieties in Great Britain, and those who have any difficulty in getting them, should write to me, enclosing please, a stamped addressed envelope for a reply.

Fir Apple – pink skinned with yellow flesh.
Kipfler – firm flesh, nutty flavour.

CHAPTER X

LEAF CROPS AS SALADS

NATURALLY it is the leafy crops that make up the bulk of the salad bowl. There are many who only think of using the lettuce in a salad, and the object of this chapter is to show that there are many other leafy crops that can be used both in the spring, summer and winter. Those who have frames, greenhouses and cloches will, of course, be able to continue the season, for as a matter of fact, the lettuce has proved to be one of the most popular glasshouse winter crops.

It must be remembered, however, that the right varieties should always be grown for the particular conditions of culture. It is no good growing an outside variety of lettuce under glass. Equally, it is useless to try and grow a summer variety of lettuce in the winter outside.

The leafy crops are useful because they are so rich in Vitamin A, Vitamin C, iron and calcium. Watercress stands particularly high in the chart issued by the National Nutrition Council, followed by mustard and cress and then lettuce. Salads are of greatest value if they are used soon after cutting, for when the lettuce and other leafy crops are kept long after being harvested, certain valuable properties are lost.

AMERICAN CRESS

The American cress was very popular during the first half of the 19th century, but it is unfortunately now almost unknown. It grows well out of doors and is one of the few salad plants available from the open ground in the winter. In flavour it is similar to ordinary cress, and has been described as a cross between mustard and cress and watercress!

The Soil
Any soil will grow American cress, providing it is lightly forked

over and plenty of finely divided organic matter is incorporated into the top 3 or 4 inches. The organic matter will hold the moisture which this plant needs and will ensure that the ground is in 'good heart'. Choose a shady situation for sowing the seed, rather than a sunny place.

Sowing the Seed
Sow the seed at any time of the year when the weather is open. The first sowing will usually be made towards the end of March in the south and at about the end of April in the north, and the last sowing of the season will be made about mid-August in the north, and early September in the south.

On a firm, but fine seed bed, draw out drills $\frac{1}{2}$ inch deep and 9 inches apart and sow the seed very thinly in these. Rake over lightly to cover and just firm over the seed rows. To keep up the supply, sowings are usually made once every three weeks from the beginning of April until the end of July.

Cultivation
If sowing is done sufficiently thinly there should be no need to thin out the plants; all that will be necessary therefore, will be regular hoeing between the rows, plus a certain amount of hand weeding in the rows. Flood the ground from time to time should the weather be dry.

The Harvesting
Cut the American cress as desired. Do not let it get too tall and lanky. It is better to do the harvesting on the young side, than to wait until it is at the seeding stage.

CHICORY

Most people know the wild chicory which grows in the chalky soils of our country and has lovely sky-blue flowers on stems 3 feet high. They are so interesting because they never remain open after twelve o'clock mid-day. The chicory, however, which we grow in our garden, is a much improved vegetable.

It is grown in the summer, the leaves not being used, but the large roots produced are dug up and forced in the heat in the dark and then the lovely yellow tender leaves are used and are very much in demand in the winter time.

Always cut the leaves of chicory just before they are required for the salad. Don't cut them an hour or so before and then leave them lying about in the light. If you do, they will toughen and will not be fit to eat.

The Soil

On the whole, chicory does best in a light soil, especially if it has been enriched with plenty of organic matter. Very heavy soils may be lightened by having sand, or flue dust or even burnt earth forked lightly into them at ½ lb. to the square yard. Poor land should be enriched with composted vegetable refuse or real well-composted farmyard manure at one barrowload to 4 square yards. A complete organic fertiliser, like a fish manure, should be raked into the top inch at 2 or 3 ounces to the square yard before sowing the seed. Carbonate of lime should be sprinkled on the surface of the soil at 3 to 4 ounces to the square yard as the final ' top dressing '.

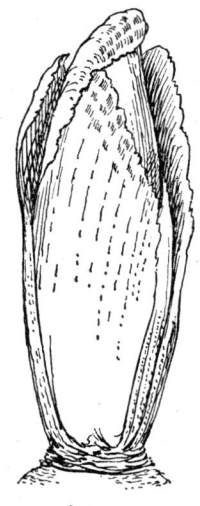

Chicory

The chicon produced as the result of forcing the root in the dark and in heat

The Sowing

The seed should not be sown until early June in the north, or mid-June in the south. Draw out the drills 15 inches apart and 1 inch deep and space the seeds out 1 foot apart in the rows. It is usual to sow three seeds at each station 1 foot apart. If each of the seeds at each station grow, the plants should be thinned out to one per station.

Cultivation

Hoe the rows regularly to keep down the weeds. The plants that start to throw up flower heads should have these removed immediately.

Harvesting

Dig up a few roots, cutting off the tops

1 inch or two inches above the crowns. Place these packed tightly, crowns upwards, in a box or pots and fill up all the nooks and crannies with soil or rotted leaves. Place this in a dark, warm spot, and cover with another box or pot, which a week later is lifted off and the roots watered well.

In a fortnight's time the roots should have begun to send up light yellow leaves, though if the temperature cannot be kept above 50 degrees F. it may take a month before the foliage is sufficiently long to cut for the salad bowl. It is best to cut when the leaves are 9 inches long – this group of hearted leaves is known as a chicon.

After the first cut, a crop of loose leaves will result three weeks or a month later, but after the second cutting the roots are useless and should then be put onto the compost heap to rot down for manure.

By bringing in batches of roots in this way, say, every three weeks, it is possible to keep up a supply of delicious heads and leaves for salad purposes until the following May. Never overdo the watering, for it is better to force the roots in a dry state than in sodden soil, or leaves.

Varieties

The commonest type of chicory to grow in this country is called Whitloof, but there is another common variety known as The Long Rooted Chicory. It is the Magdeburg variety whose roots are used for making coffee.

CORN SALAD

The corn salad when growing looks something like the forget-me-not, except that it does not have blue flowers. It is sometimes called Lamb's Lettuce, and is of the greatest value in the winter time. It grows excellently under cloches, and in the gardens of The Good Gardeners' Association at Arkley it is usually kept available throughout the winter.

The Soil

This is a crop that will grow on almost any soil but it does best on land rich in organic matter. Well-composted vegetable refuse or medium grade sedge peat should be forked in 2 inches or so deep at the rate of one good barrowload to 4 square yards, as well as meat and bone meal, hoof and horn meal or a fish manure at 4 to 5 ounces to the square yard. The surface of the soil should be dusted with carbonate of lime afterwards.

The Sowing

Get the surface of the soil fine and level by alternate treading and raking. Sow the seeds in drills 1 foot apart and $\frac{3}{4}$ inch deep. Place 3 seeds in stations 9 inches apart along the drills and thin the seedlings down to one if all 3 seedlings grow. Transplant the thinnings to other rows if necessary. Rake the soil level. Sow in mid-June, mid-July, mid-August and mid-September, and to ensure that plants are not killed, even in the south, cover the rows with cloches from the end of September onwards.

Cultivation

Hoe regularly between the rows, until the winter makes this impossible. Water well in the summer months if the weather is very dry and the plants seem to ' hang fire '.

Harvesting

The leaves may be cut singly or, if preferred, a whole plant may be pulled up and used at once. It is possible to start to pull from the time the plants have made 4 to 5 leaves, though it is better to delay until a nice little bushy plant has developed.

Varieties

There are only two types, the Round Leaved and the Regence, which has pointed leaves.

DANDELION

The cultivated Dandelion is as valuable as Chicory. It is grown in the same manner. The roots are dug up in the winter as advised for chicory and are forced in a similar manner but do not produce heads, only leaves. When blanched they have not got a bitter taste and so are much liked.

Green Batavian Endive

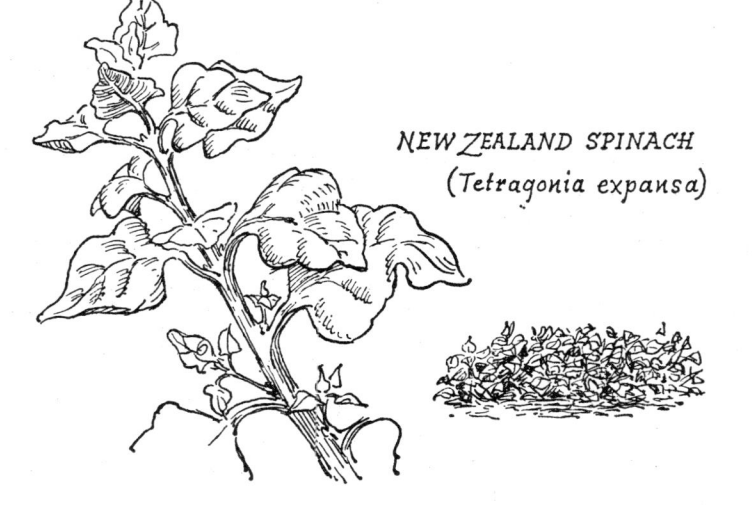

Moss Curled Endive

NEW ZEALAND SPINACH
(Tetragonia expansa)

ENDIVE

Endive is a salad plant that is far too little grown, being ideal for the winter, especially when properly blanched. It is a plant that is always best eaten raw. Most gardeners aim to sow in June and plant out in August and then start to blanch in September or early October, or you can sow *in situ* and thin out. This is the easier method.

The Soil

Whatever the soil in the garden is like, it should be enriched with plenty of finely divided organic matter, such as sedge peat, in order to grow endive really well. This organic material might also be in the form of composted leaves, powdery compost, or similar material. It is best to fork this in to the top 3 or 4 inches at the rate of $\frac{1}{2}$ lb. to the square yard. In addition, use a good fish manure or a meat and bone meal at 3 ounces or 4 ounces to the square yard. If the soil is very hungry, then well-composted vegetable refuse or old well-rotted farmyard manure may be dug in at the rate of one good barrowload to 12 square yards.

The Sowing

Prepare a fine seed bed by alternate raking and treading. By this means the soil will be got down into really fine particles. Draw out the drills 6 inches apart and $\frac{1}{2}$ inch deep and sprinkle the seed in very thinly. Rake over lightly to cover. 15th June is usually a convenient date. When the seedlings are 1 inch high, prick them out to a further bed 6 inches by 3 inches and then 3 weeks to a month later, plant them out into their permanent rows 1 foot square.

Some prefer to sow seeds in threes, 12 inches to 15 inches apart along the drills where the plants are going to grow, thinning the seedlings down to one if all three grow. The great thing in either case, is to make certain the plants never suffer from lack of water. Always try and grow endive in full sun.

Cultivation

Keep the rows hoed regularly, apply sedge peat alongside the plants during the summer to help to conserve moisture. Give regular floodings once a week should the weather be very dry.

The Blanching

When the plants are fully grown, anything from three to four months after seed sowing, some method of blanching should be adopted. Method No. 1 consists of covering the plants with a flower-pot upside down, filling up the drainage hole with some clay or with a stone so as to exclude all light. Method No. 2 is to coat the inside of cloches thickly with whitewash or mud and put them over the plants, closing up the ends of the row with sheets of glass treated in a similar manner. Method No. 3 is to lift the plants in succession and plant them in soil in a cellar or darkened outhouse, or even to plant them closely in a frame, keeping the lights closed and covering them with sacking.

When the foliage of endive has turned yellowy white it must be used as soon as possible. No watering should be done for a week before blanching.

Continuity

For continuity throughout the winter, it is advisable to make four sowings, the first in mid-June and the next two at three-weekly intervals.

Varieties

There are two main types: (1) The Moss Curled, or Improved Green Curled, which has crinkly leaves; (2) The Batavian, or Green Batavian, which grows leaves more like a lettuce. The former is usually the more popular of the two – but the latter looks like the lettuce so beginners prefer it.

LETTUCE

The gardener should aim at producing lettuces all the year round. This he can easily do if, in addition to his outdoor sowings for the spring, summer and autumn, he can grow a certain amount under cloches, in frames or in a cool greenhouse. There are, of course, two main types of lettuce, the cos and the cabbage, though the cross, which is usually known as semi-cos, is particularly useful, especially if a good strain like Osmaston Gem is grown.

Fortunately all types of lettuce need a similar form of cultivation, and two great mistakes made with this crop are usually: (1) The sowing of too many seeds at one particular time with the result that there are too many lettuces at one time of the year, and none at the next; and (2) transplanting too late. Lettuces should always be put out into their new positions when they are only 1 inch or so high.

The Soil

Much finely divided organic matter, such as sedge peat, should be forked into the top 2 or 3 inches of soil to be used for growing lettuces. This ensures aeration, helps to retain moisture, and eventually gives the sort of food the lettuce needs. Land that has not been manured for some time should have well-composted powdery vegetable refuse applied at the rate of 1 barrowload to 4 square yards.

Fish manure or meat and bone meals are a good dressing, consisting of 2 ounces of meat and bone meal, 2 ounces fish manure, $\frac{1}{2}$ ounce precipated bone phosphates and 2 ounces wood ashes per square yard. I have had excellent results with this special mixture.

Sowing the Seeds

There are four main periods of the year for sowing seed.
1. In frames or under cloches in early February to plant out early in April;
2. Out of doors in March or early April for the summer;
3. In the open in August for use in the late winter;
4. Seed sown in mid-October under cloches for cutting in March and April.

It is possible also, to sow seeds under cloches in January and again in February.

Directly March comes, the aim should be to sow a pinch of lettuce seed once a fortnight throughout the year until late in August. If the plants are required, then they can be put out, and if they are not required little seed has been wasted. The great thing is to keep planting and thus never be without lettuces – the mainstay of the salad bowl – all the year through. Care has to be taken to sow different varieties for different seasons of the year; Arctic King, for instance, is a variety that will live outside during the winter, while Gotte à Forcer is a tender type that has done best in the hotbed frame during the winter months.

Lettuces can, of course, be sown where they are to grow. This is a common method with market gardeners, especially in the case of sowings made outside in August and September. In this case the seed is sown thinly in rows 1 foot apart and the plants are thinned out to 8 inches apart either before the winter sets in, or in the north, after the hard weather has passed.

When sowing under glass, a temperature of about 65 degrees F. should be aimed at. The compost used should be the Alex 'No-Soil' Compost which any good horticultural sundriesman can let you have.

The seed box should be well drained and should be filled with soil to within $\frac{1}{2}$ inch of the top. The seed should then be sown very thinly, the seeds being covered with a sifting of a little more of the same compost and made firm. If the boxes are covered with a sheet of glass and a piece of brown paper, correct germination will be ensured.

Water the boxes after sowing, but not again until the seedlings are well through. As soon as the plants are 1 inch high they should be transplanted 1 inch square to further boxes, using a similar compost. The plants should be hardened off by standing them out in a frame, and if the seed has been sown in February, it should be ready to plant out in the south, late in March and in the north, about the middle of April. To ensure that there are no losses, it is advisable to cover these early plantings with cloches for several weeks.

In the Open

Seeds may be sown in the open in rows 1 foot apart, any time from the beginning of March (in the south) and from the beginning of April (in the north) onwards, depending on the district. The plants are thinned to 10 inches apart, and the thinnings can be transplanted to other beds if necessary. Successive sowings will be made every fortnight or three weeks.

The outdoor winter lettuces are sown early in August in the north and mid-August in the south, varieties like Arctic King and Imperial being used, or if a cos lettuce is preferred, Bath Cos. These varieties will usually live out of doors without any covering and come into use after the turn of the warm weather in the spring.

In the Frames

Those who have frames or cloches will make a sowing in October, during the early part in the north and about the middle of the month in the south. On mild days, the frames can be left open after the plants are through, being closed down an hour before sunset to bottle up the day's warmth. The lettuces should stand 9 inches apart in the frames if they are to grow at their best.

Cultivation

The earlier lettuces are transplanted, the better. They must be handled carefully for they are very tender. They should never be left out of the ground longer than possible for their roots dry out quickly, and they should always be planted shallowly. Hoeing should be done regularly between the rows — care being taken not to cut the plants during hoeing at any time. It is never advisable to go on the land in the winter when it is wet, so avoid surface cultivation when the ground is sticky.

Cos lettuce do not heart as easily as cabbage and they are usually tied round the middle with raffia when they have made about three-quarters of their growth. The cos types, too, are said to need far more moisture. It is usual only to make two sowings of cos lettuce, one in the spring and one in the summer. The semi-cos types, however, may be sown at any time.

Harvesting

The lettuces should be cut as required, and before there is any sign of bolting. It is better to cut early in the morning and bring the lettuces in while they are still cool; they can then be stood in water in a cool shady place until required.

Varieties

All the Year Round is one of the best types for spring sowing; as is Webb's Wonderful, which has curly, crinkly leaves and grows very large. It is a favourite of the Author's. Continuity is probably the best for sowing early in March. The best cos to grow is Paris White; for August sowing in the open, Arctic King is most suited for the north, and Improved Trocadero (Unrivalled) for the south.

A good winter cos lettuce is Winter Density, while Little Gem is an excellent semi-cos. For September and October sowing under cloches I like Attractie; and for January and February sowings and frames, Gotte à Forcer. Cheshunt Early Giant is a good winter lettuce for the greenhouse.

MUSTARD AND CRESS

Mustard and cress are usually classed together and eaten together, though of course, they can just as easily be eaten separately. Where it is desired to cut these crops at the same time, the cress should be sown three days before the mustard, for the latter is the much quicker grower.

Sowing the Seed

For a winter supply, the crop can be grown in boxes under glass, but in the spring and summer it can be sown, if preferred, out of doors. Some growers put a layer of fine sedge peat on top of the soil and sow the seeds on top of the sedge peat, and so the seedlings grow free from soil and are not gritty. It is possible to sow the seed on damp sacking laid on the soil. This also prevents grittiness.

Rape can be used instead of mustard and this has the advantage of not going soft in hot weather. As rape grows at the same pace as cress it should be sown at the same time as the cress, and not three days later as in the case of mustard.

One pound of mustard seed is needed for every 2 square yards sown and $\frac{3}{4}$ lb. of rape or cress seed. In all cases the seeds germinate best in darkness, and so sacking should be thrown over, or the seed should be covered with brown paper. If grown in boxes, it is often advisable to place these under the benches of the greenhouse and to bring them into the light five days after the seeds have germinated.

Harvesting

Mustard and cress should always be cut with a pair of scissors, as, if pulled up by the roots, the salad is apt to be gritty. As it is possible to sow all the year round, it should be possible to harvest all the year round.

Damping Off

One of the troubles of this crop is that the seedlings are apt to damp off when they are young, but this can be prevented if the soil is sterilised before using by heating it up to 220 degrees F. or if it is watered well with plenty of really boiling water.

SPINACH

Spinach is normally eaten cooked, but it is very delicious when eaten raw if it is grown quickly in soil rich in organic matter. The annual or summer spinach is better eaten raw than the perennial or New Zealand spinach, though all three have been used.

The great advantage of spinach is that it is rich in iron, calcium and phosphorus as well as Vitamins A, B_1 and B_2.

The Soil

Whatever soil is used should be well drained, and light soil should have plenty of organic matter forked into it to enrich the top 2 inches. Use really well-rotted seaweed, composted leaf-mould, or sedge peat at, say, 2 lb. to the square yard. When forking the land over in the spring, well-composted vegetable refuse should be incorporated at one good barrowload to 4 square yards.

A fish manure with a 6 per cent potash content, or a good meat and bone meal, or better still, a combination of the two should be applied as a top dressing before seed sowing, at the rate of 4 to 5 ounces to the square yard, and this should be lightly raked in. The plants may be encouraged when they are growing by applying dried blood along the rows at 1 ounce to the yard run.

Sowing the Seed

There are two main periods for sowing the seed: (a) the summer spinach which is usually put in once a fortnight from the begining of March onwards, and (b) the winter spinach which is usually sown once a fortnight from the beginning of August to the middle of September.

In the case of the summer spinach, the drills should be 1 foot apart and 1 inch deep and sowing should be so thinly done that there will be few plants to pull out when they are thinned to 6 inches apart a few weeks later. It is better to make a number of short sowings in the normal garden than one long sowing. As the weather gets warmer, the sowing should be made in the shadier parts of the garden, as this will prevent them going to seed too quickly.

The seed of winter spinach is best sown in raised beds, say 5 feet wide and 3 inches above the level of the soil around. This gives extra drainage and helps to keep the beds dry. The rows should be made 9 inches apart and the seedlings thinned 4 inches apart.

Cultivation

The great thing with spinach in the summer, is to keep it growing and prevent it going to seed. This can be done by: (1) giving thorough soakings with water if the weather is dry, and this is available, (2) hoeing regularly between the rows, (3) applying mulchings of sedge peat alongside the rows.

It helps tremendously also, if there is plenty of sedge peat in the top 2 or 3 inches, especially if it is thoroughly dampened first.

The winter spinach will need protection and should be covered with continuous cloches or, if these are not available, straw or bracken. Winter spinach should not be hoed during the damp weather or when the soil is sticky.

Harvesting

The summer spinach can be picked as desired. Many people

pull up a whole plant when it is young and tender, and this is a very good plan where the leaves are to be used for salad purposes. Winter spinach, on the other hand, should not be picked too hard. The largest leaves should be taken each time, singly.

Types

For the winter, Long Standing Prickly. This may be sown in the spring as well as in August if desired. For the summer, Improved Round Victoria and Monarch Long Standing.

WATERCRESS

Watercress is one of the most popular salads both in the winter and summer. It is rich in vitamins and is valuable from a medicinal point of view, owing to its oil and mineral content. It can be grown out of doors in the summer, and in the winter a supply can be kept up in the cold frame. In the normal way, of course, it is grown in special water-covered beds, but it can be grown in trenches out of doors in any ordinary garden. A shady situation should be chosen; a dark, damp corner where nothing else will grow is quite ideal.

Preparation

A trench should be dug out 2 feet deep and 2 or 3 feet wide, in the bottom of which should be placed a 9-inch layer of well-rotted composted vegetable refuse. This should be given a thorough soaking; leave the trench for a fortnight, giving it three or four gallons of water each day per yard run during this time. Then place 4 inches of good soil over the compost and press firm.

Sowing the Seed

If preferred, seeds of watercress may be sown in the soil at the bottom of the trench, 3 seeds to each station, 8 inches apart. If each of the seeds germinate, the seedlings should be thinned down to one per station. During the time the seeds are germinating, keep the trench dark by covering over with old sacks, on a framework of poles or bamboos. When the plants are through, remove the sacking and give a good flooding.

Planting

The watercress plants should be put out into the soil 8 inches square. These may be cuttings of watercress from the ordinary bunches bought from the greengrocer, some of which may have little roots on them.

Cultivation

Keep the soil free from weeds by hand weeding, until the plants cover the bottom. Never allow the soil to become dry. It is a good plan to water every day through the fine rose of a watering can, unless the weather be rainy. When the plants are about 6 inches high, pinch out the leading shoot so as to cause them to become bushy. Never allow plants to flower, but cut them back and start them growing again. It is quite a good plan to make 3 or 4 small beds, each one a month after the other, rather than making one large bed. It is thus that continuity can be assured.

CHAPTER XI

THE BULB SALADS

No one ought to neglect growing onions, for they are one of the most useful additions to salads. They contain Vitamins B_1 and C, and a certain quantity of calcium and iron. A supply can be kept up for salad purposes throughout the year, if alternative types like chives, Welsh onions and Rocambole onions are grown. The onion is one of the oldest plants in history, being mentioned in the Bible in the 11th Chapter of Numbers.

The main types of onions which can be grown to be eaten raw, either fresh or in pickles, are (1) the spring-sown onions, (2) autumn-sown onions, (3) salad onions, (4) Welsh onions, (5) potato onions, (6) tree onions and (7) rocamboles. The last have been described as a mild form of garlic.

The Soil

Onions prefer a rich sandy loam which can be easily cultivated. They can, of course, be grown on clay soils if these are lightened by the forking in of sand, sedge peat or burnt soil.

The soil must be prepared properly by forking it over to make the surface fine and loose. This should be done a week before the seed is sown. Well-composted powdery vegetable waste should be applied on the surface of the soil in the early winter at the rate of 1 good barrowload to 4 square yards. In the spring, before sowing the seed, a good fish manure with a 6 per cent potash content should be raked in at the rate of 3 ounces to the square yard. Wood ashes may be used in addition, if available, at the rate of $\frac{1}{2}$ lb. to the square yard.

Sowing the Seed

Before sowing the seed the soil should be trodden to make the bed firm unless the earth is a very heavy clay. This work should never be done when the soil is sticky. When the soil is in the right condition, i.e. when the top inch or so is almost dry, drills mays be drawn out ¼ inch deep and 1 foot apart. This should be towards the end of March in the south and the middle of April in the north, though in parts of the south-west sowings may even be made as early as February. It is most important to sow thinly. After sowing, cover up the drills by a light raking and then tread along the rows to firm the soil.

Cultivation

Hoe regularly along the rows to keep down weeds, drawing the soil away from the plants, rather than up to them. When the plants are 3 inches high, apply a Derris and Pyrethrum dust in between the rows at the rate of 1 ounce to the yard run, to keep away the Onion Fly* and thus prevent attacks of maggots. Ten days later thinnings may be done to 3 inches apart and a few weeks later again to 6 inches apart, the thinnings being used for salad purposes.

Should the weather be very dry, regular waterings or floodings should be given along the rows, these being discontinued after the middle of August. Mulchings of lawn mowings or damp sedge peat may be made along the rows also.

Harvesting

Allow the bulbs to ripen naturally, but help them by bending the tops over at the neck about the middle of August in the north, and about the end of August or the beginning of September in the south. It is after this that the necks commence to shrink, and a fortnight or so later the onions may be lifted out of the soil and left on the surface of the ground to dry off. This drying-off process may be continued by taking the bulbs and laying them on a gravel or cinder path upside down in the sun.

The onions may be stored by stringing them up on ropes and hanging them under the shelter of the eaves of a building. It may be preferred to store them on slatted shelves in a cool house. The main thing is not to allow the onions to get damp, for then they tend to rot off or start into growth again.

---

* See the note on Carrot Fly control on Page 109.

Types
Suitable types and varieties for sowing in the spring are Bedfordshire Champion, Lancastrian, Ailsa Craig and Unwin's Exhibition.

AUTUMN-SOWN ONIONS

The difference between the autumn-sown onions and the spring-sown ones, lies largely in the fact that from the autumn-sown onions we get earlier bulbs to use in the kitchen. These, on the other hand, do not keep so well as the spring-sown onions.

The Soil
Unlike the spring-sown onions there is no reason to dig in compost for the autumn-sown onions should follow a well-manured crop such as early peas, early potatoes or early carrots. It is therefore only necessary to rake the ground down finely, add a fish manure with an organic base at 3 ounces to the square yard, draw out the drills and sow the seed.

Sowing the Seed
Sow during the latter part of July or the middle of August. On the whole, the further north the earlier the sowing. Make the rows 1 foot apart and aim to sow the seeds $\frac{1}{2}$ inch apart. Cover as advised for spring-sown onions.

Cultivation
Hoe between the rows till the winter makes this impossible, and then in the spring start to hoe again. In April thin out to 6 inches between the plants, transplanting the thinnings into further rows at similar distances.

Harvesting
As advised for spring-sown onions, about the middle of July.

Type
Unwin's Reliance.

SALAD ONIONS

These should be sown in exactly similar manner to the autumn-sown onions and at approximately the same time. The rows, however, may be 9 inches apart and the drills somewhat wider than usual. No thinning need be done for the plants are pulled out as required for salads. The seed is sown fairly thickly.

Types
Good varieties are White Lisbon, which is sometimes subject to disease, and where this is the case, New Queen should be grown instead.

PICKLING ONIONS

Pickling onions should be grown in poor soil. It is only necessary to rake the soil over level and then to broadcast the seed evenly over the surface, raking it in lightly. It is best to sow about the middle of April and not to thin at all. A certain amount of hand weeding has to be done, however. Little pickling bulbs will be formed in July and these can be forked up as advised in the case of spring-sown onions to ripen off, first of all on the surface of the ground and then on a hard path or concrete yard.

Types
Varieties which make excellent picklers are Barla and The Queen.

WELSH ONIONS

The Welsh onion came originally from Siberia and is a kind of herbaceous perennial. It is very hardy, there being two main types, the Red and the White. When growing, the Welsh onion plant looks like a bunch of spring onions all

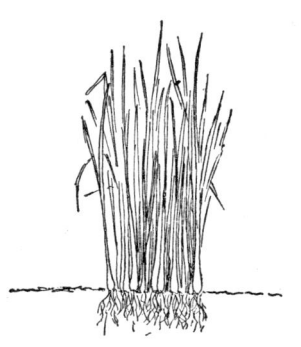

Welsh Onion
A Perennial Onion.

attached to the same root. It is possible to pull off these salad-like onions almost any time of the year.

They will grow on any soil and under almost any conditions. Young plants may be obtained by division of the older plants in the spring and autumn, and each plant when put out easily produces 30 or 40 further plants around it. It is possible to raise plants by sowing seed in July or August.

The perennial onion makes quite a good edging plant to any vegetable garden and if planted in rows should be set out about 1 foot square.

The onions in a cluster on the tall stem.

Tree Onions

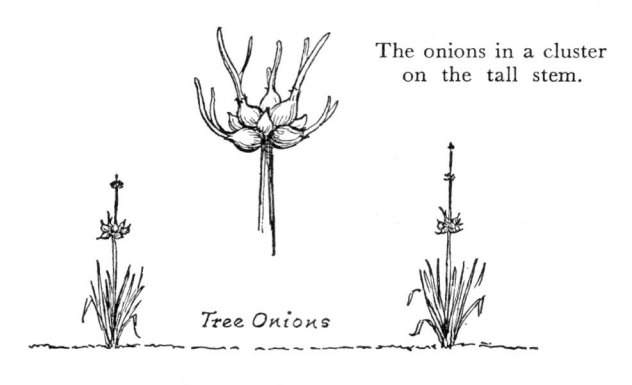

What they look like when growing.

TREE ONIONS

The tree onion is interesting in that it has bulbs at the roots and further little bulbs at the top of the stems. Both can be used and are very delicious. There may be over a dozen small onions on the top of each stem if the plants are well grown. It is these bulbs which should be planted out in shallow drills early in April in rows 18 inches apart, the bulbs being 6 inches apart in the rows. The plants usually need support because of the weight of the little onions they bear.

Care should be taken to see that the soil is kept firm around the plants for the first three weeks after planting. The tops may grow 3 feet high.

POTATO ONIONS

This has been called the underground onion and is usually grown like the shallot. The ground should be prepared as for the ordinary onion, the planting being done in March, or in the south-west as early as February. The rows should be 1 foot apart and the plants 9 inches apart in the rows, the plants being buried just below the surface.

Earth the plants up when the growths are of a good size and numerous clusters of onions will be formed. If the weather is very dry, give plenty of water, but withhold this as the bulbs begin to ripen. Fork up about the second week of August, the bulbs being left on the surface to ripen off.

ROCAMBOLE

This is similar to the Welsh onion, except that is is a native of Europe and is very popular in Lancashire, Yorkshire and parts of Scotland and Ireland. In some parts it is called the Sand Leek, though it is said that its name ' Rocambole ' comes from the Anglo-Saxon name meaning ' onion on rocks '! It is very similar to the garlic but is milder in flavour. The bulbs or cloves, as they are called, should be planted in rows 8 inches apart, 6 inches apart in the rows and 2 inches deep.

There is nothing to be done, other than hoe regularly between the rows to keep down weeds.

SHALLOTS

The shallot is one of the easiest of vegetables to grow and is excellent for pickling purposes. It grows well on any soil though, if anything, it prefers a well-drained light loam. The bulbs should be planted as early as possible, in the south in January or early February, and in the north in March. The rows should be 12 inches apart and the bulbs should be spaced out 6 inches apart.

Use up any odd places, such as the edging of the allotment or garden. Firm the soil and then push the bulbs in to half their depth. Remove any dead tops or loose skins for worms like to draw these parts down into the soil. A fortnight after planting firm again.

Hoe regularly but not deeply. Take care not to cut the bulbs. Hoe away from the bulbs, rather than up to them. In July the shallots will start to ripen off, and about the second or third week they may be lifted onto the surface of the soil to dry off. After a few days they may be placed on a hard path or concrete yard and turned over two or three times to make certain they are really dry. They should then be stored so that the air can circulate around them in a dark cool place.

Types
The best type is the True Red or Danish Yellow Shallot. Latterly the Russian Shallot, sometimes called the Jersey or Dutch Shallot, has been used and this throws a much larger bulb, coppery red in colour.

CHIVES

These useful plants are usually planted in groups, or they can be used to make a nice edging. The leaves or 'grass' are the part which is used, picked as required and chopped up whenever an onion flavour is wanted.

Propagation
This is done, simply by dividing the clumps every two or three years.

Cultivation
The decorative mauve flowers should be picked off the moment they appear.

GARLIC

The garlic plant consists of a 'bulb' which is really made up of numerous bulbets known as 'cloves'. These have papery scales between them and are enclosed in a thick white skin which holds them all together.

The Planting

The separate cloves are planted 2 inches down early in spring in a sunny bed.

The bulbs are lifted when the leaves die down in July or August and should be dried in the sun for a few days and then hung in a dry shed.

CHAPTER XII

VARIOUS TYPES OF CELERY

CELERY is very useful to the man or woman who is keen on eating vegetables raw, but it is a crop which takes a great deal of growing. Ordinary celery can be used from October onwards as a salad, either being eaten alone, or with cheese (a delicacy in which so many delight), or by being cut up and mixed with other salads. It is foolish to say, as some people do, that celery is not worth growing because it is so often frozen in the trenches and goes rotten in March when a thaw sets in.

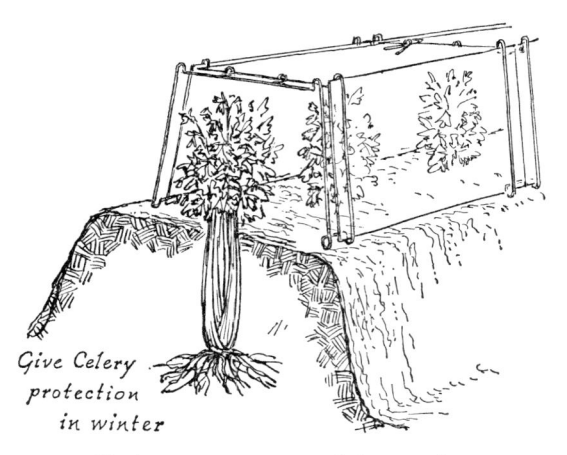

Give Celery protection in winter

Cloches are put on top of the trenches.

To keep celery growing in the winter time, it is only necessary to cover the rows with cloches or frames laid on their sides made into 'tents' – and this not only helps to keep the frost out, but also prevents the rain from seeping down into the hearts of celery and so starting the rot. It is a very good idea to put bracken, straw, or similar material over the plants, or to take this on either side of the trenches with the idea of keeping the frost out.

Self-bleaching or dwarf celery can be ready in August and is grown on the level of the ground, or on the flat as it is called, but ordinary celery is best grown in trenches. The very preparation of the trenches has a beneficial effect on the soil, and therefore where celery is grown, the ground is improved and becomes better for the production of other crops in the years that follow.

The Conditions for Growth

Naturally, because it grows in trenches, a deep soil is advisable for celery, and market gardeners who go in for this crop prefer a soil rich in peat, such as is found in parts of Lancashire and Cheshire. There is no need to lime for celery, and in fact, soils that are slightly acid seem to suit this crop better. As there is a tendency for plants to go to seed if the soil is at all dry, it is advisable to fork plenty of organic matter into the ground. In counties like Lincolnshire, celery is grown on land which has a high water table.

Preparing the Trenches

It is usual to prepare trenches about 12 inches deep and 15 inches wide for a single row. The soil which is dug out to form the trench should be thrown out at either side of it in equal proportions to form ridges equal in height, the distance being 2 feet 6 inches between the trenches.

Having dug out the trench or trenches, well-composted refuse should be placed in the bottom to a depth of at least 6 inches and should be forked in. A good treading should then be given to ensure that the bottom of the trench is firm, and on top of this firmed mixture of soil and manure, a 4 inch depth of good soil should be placed. After treading this in, a fish manure at 4 to 5 ounces to the yard run, or a good meat and bone meal at a similar rate should be applied along the bottom of the trench before the surface is raked over. Further applications of such manures may be given once a month from July to the end of September. What is needed is a good complete fertiliser with an organic base.

The Sowing

Don't make the mistake of sowing the seed too early. If the sowing is done about the middle of February, good sticks are ready to use about the beginning of September. Such sowing has to be done, however, in boxes filled with John Innes Compost or the 'No-Soil' Compost in a greenhouse at a temperature of about 60 degrees F. The main sowing should be carried out in March, over a hotbed or in a frame or cool greenhouse. The hotbed can be made by treading down horse manure in a frame till it reaches a depth of 1 foot. It should then be covered with 4 inches of good soil.

To ensure that there is no disease in the soil, it should be soaked when in position with a 2 per cent solution of formaldehyde, being covered afterwards with sacks or old sacking, thus keeping in the fumes. If 1 pint of formaldehyde is dissolved in 6 gallons of water, it is ample for a frame 6 feet by 4 feet. Five days later, remove the sacks and fork the soil over well, to release the fumes. Fork again the following day and in two or three days' time the soil will be ready to sow with seed. In such a frame, in addition to celery plants, it is possible to raise leeks and any members of the brassica family desired. Onions could also be raised in the same way.

A pinch of celery seed will usually provide all the plants required for the normal garden, ¼ ounce of seed producing well over 1,000 plants. Sprinkle the seed over the surface of the ground and rake in lightly and then press with a wooden presser to firm. Water through the fine rose of a can and close the frame down for a week or so. If the weather is frosty in the night time, cover the frame with old sacks.

Directly the seedlings are through, give a little air during the day on all suitable occasions. Gradually increase the amount of air so that by the middle of April the lights can be removed altogether on the warm days. When the plants are 2 inches high they should be transplanted to further frames or to warm sheltered beds in a sunny position in the open.

Later Sowings

It is possible to make later sowings, either during the second week of March, or the second week of April. In the former case, it should be done in a frame and in the latter case, in the open on a sunny border.

The Planting Out

When the plants are about 4 inches high they may be put out into the trenches 1 foot apart. They should be lifted carefully with a trowel, with as much soil attached to the roots as possible, a good hole being made with the trowel so as to take all the roots without 'bunching them up' in any way. After planting, the soil should be made firm around them and the trench should then be given a thorough soaking with water.

The Cultivating

It will be necessary to keep the bottom of the trenches moist during most of the summer. This will have to be done by regular waterings. Once a month, feeds will be given with some complete fertiliser as advised earlier on.

Side growths developing from the base of the celery plants should be removed when seen, and it will be necessary to spray the plants from June onwards with Liquid Derris plus extract of Pyrethrum to keep down the Celery Fly, and often with Bordeaux Mixture from July onwards, to keep down the Celery Blight. Celery is no easy crop to grow, being prone to these two troubles. It is not considered by most gardeners an inexpensive crop to grow either.

Earthing up should be done from the middle of August onwards, a start being made, as a rule, when the plants are about 15 inches high. One hand should be grasped firmly around each plant while the soil is being put into position. This prevents any soil getting in between the stems, which is important. A good plan is to fork or chop the soil down finely an hour before it is to be used, for by this method the earth warms up somewhat. It is never advisable to earth higher than the base of the leaves each time.

The Harvesting

Eight weeks after the first earthing-up, the sticks should be sufficiently well blanched to be used.

Types

There are the red, pink and white types of celery. The pink and red are on the whole the hardier, and the white the most delicious. A good white is, because of its earliness, Exhibition White, and because it is fairly resistant to blight; a good pink is Superb Pink, a large early; while among the best reds undoubtedly are Standard Bearer and Exhibition Red, both of which grow solid sticks of good size.

SELF-BLEACHING CELERY

Self-bleaching celery should be grown by those who do not want the trouble of preparing trenches. It is, however, quick growing, and is usually ready to use in August and September. It will not last until Christmas time. The plants can be raised in a similar manner as advised for ordinary celery and when they are 3 or 4 inches high and have been hardened off, they may be planted out in rows 12 inches apart, giving 13 inches apart in the rows. Some of the dwarfer varieties need to be no closer than 12 inches by 9 inches. Dig the ground over well first of all, incorporating plenty of farmyard manure or well-rotted vegetable refuse. Soak the ground after planting and hoe well 2 or 3 days later.

Though termed the self-bleaching celery, it is always better to help the plants to blanch properly by placing plenty of straw among them, or by wrapping sacking around the bed as a kind of fence and laying other sacks over the tops of the plants. These sacks should be kept from pressing down on the plants, by having a series of posts and wires or strings stretched from end to end of the plot, 2 inches or so higher than the plants.

Types

There are many kinds of self-bleaching celery advertised, the best of which is probably Lathom Blanching, a yellowy white dwarf of excellent flavour.

GREEN CELERY
or American Celery

A very delicious American Celery which doesn't need earthing up. The seed is sown in February, as for other celeries. The plants when ready are planted out in June or July in rich compost-fed ground. Put plenty of compost in a layer 1 inch deep on the soil and plant out the celery 1 foot square. The green celery grown in this way is ready for use from September onwards.

The variety, Greensleeves, is particularly delicious.

CELERIAC

Some people would put celeriac into the chapter dealing with unusual vegetables, but it is much better known now than it was. It has been called the Turnip-Rooted celery for it grows similarly to that vegetable and yet tastes just like the heart of celery. It can be used sliced into salads and has many advantages for it can be grown on the surface of the ground in areas where it would be impossible to do ordinary celery well. No blanching has to be done. Celeriac will keep for 6 months after it is fully grown.

The plants should be raised in the same way as advised for celery, being put out when 3 or 4 inches high late in May or early in June. The rows should be 18 inches apart and the plants 15 to 18 inches in the rows. See that the soil is well enriched with organic matter before planting, for like celery, celeriac dislikes dryness at the roots and organic matter will act as a sponge and help to hold the moisture.

Keep the rows regularly hoed, and if possible apply grass cuttings or lawn mowings in and around the plant, to act as a mulch. Once a fortnight from the end of June onwards, give a light feed of liquid manure, or sprinkle a fish fertiliser along the rows at the rate of $\frac{1}{2}$ ounce to the yard run. Side growths seen developing from the base of the plant should always be removed.

A fortnight before harvesting, draw the soil up to the rows

so as to cover the hearts, up to the foliage. This will help to blanch the top of the roots.

The celeriac may either be dug up and stored in a shed or outhouse or may be clamped as advised for other root crops.

Good types are Giant Prague, which grows a large bulb, and Paris Ameliore, which is said to be of better quality.

Celeriac

The Turnip-rooted Celery

CHAPTER XIII

CUCUMBERS

THE culture of cucumbers is one of the oldest arts known, and this salad has been popular in China and Egypt for thousands of years.

There are the three main types of Cucumbers – the frame – the ridge – and the apple. The frame types are those that are normally grown in greenhouses, or frames. They can be subdivided, because there are varieties like Telegraph which do better in the greenhouse, and others like Conqueror which do better in a frame. Then there are the ridge cucumbers which grow happily out of doors without being covered in any way, providing they are not planted out until all fear of frost has passed. Lastly there is the Apple Cucumber which can be grown under glass or in the open and which bears round fruits, about the size of a large apple.

Seed Sowing

Seeds can be sown at any time from early January onwards in 3 inch pots – a seed being placed point downwards in the centre of each pot. The bottom of the pot should be well crocked and covered for 1 inch with a few rough pieces of sedge peat. After sowing, the seeds are covered with $\frac{1}{2}$ inch of the same compost and then well watered, with water at the same temperature as the house. The pots can be placed on a shelf in a house where bottom heat can be obtained. Seed sowing can be carried out in ordinary seed-boxes, usually 48 seeds to a box – $\frac{1}{4}$ inch of compost covering the seed. These boxes are then placed in the greenhouse, and a piece of glass placed over the boxes. The temperature of the house at this stage should never be allowed to fall below 70 degrees F. at night time. Use the Alex 'No-Soil' Compost which you can get ready to use from any good Horticultural Sundriesman.

Potting Up

In ten days to a fortnight, the plants should be ready to be transferred to their permanent beds, but if these are not ready they may be shifted into a 5 inch pot temporarily, the soil for the compost being similar. This compost should be at the same temperature as the house. Cucumbers differ from most plants in that they should not be potted firmly. Each plant should be inserted up to the seed leaf. A good soaking is again necessary. Watering after need only be done when the soil appears dry, for good root development cannot take place in continually wet soil.

Staking

After a week the plants will need support, and an 18 inch piece of bamboo should be inserted into the soil, to which the

Cucumbers growing on their prepared beds – note the mounds in which the young plants are set.

cucumber stem should be loosely tied in order to allow for development.

The House

A type of glasshouse which seems to suit cucumbers is 15 feet wide, with 3 feet rise to the gutter-board. The house should be preferably, in a sunny position and protected from the north and east cold winds. Hot-water pipes will be necessary for bottom heat, and it is wise to have the heat as near the cucumber-bed as possible. Ventilation is rarely necessary, and air should be admitted with great caution. Ventilators, if used, should be closed quite early in the afternoon at all seasons. Towards July, a slight ventilation may be given, particularly on the leeward side, just to change the air in the house.

The Bed

It is very important to ensure good drainage all the time, and water must be able to get away quickly. Clinkers may be used for drainage under the main bed. Recently I have made up my cucumber-beds on bales of straw.

Any organic material of an open texture which will allow for drainage makes a satisfactory base. The beds should be made 2 weeks before planting, if possible, and should be at least 1 foot 6 inches wide at the base and 1 foot wide at the top. On the bed, mounds should be made about 3 feet apart consisting of a good rich compost, 3 parts good loam, 1 part old compost. These mounds should be made moderately firm, and so arranged as to allow drips from rafters to fall between the plants. The whole house should be heated for a week to ensure all the soil, etc. being warmed through before introducing the young plants.

Transferring the Plants

When the plants are 6 inches-9 inches high they may be transferred to their permanent beds; the greatest care should be taken that they are not chilled in so doing. The pots should be immersed in the middle of each mound, and should remain in the holes thus made for 24 hours before knocking the ball of soil out, and the plants should be 3 inches below the surface of the bed. Watering may then be carried out, a gallon being given to every 3 mounds only. A stake must now be provided for the purpose of training the new growth to the wires or trellis, as described before.

Temperature

The atmosphere of a cucumber house must never feel dry, and a brisk temperature should be maintained at all time.

Damping down by syringing must be done frequently, Sundays included. The night temperature should be 70 degrees F. and in the daytime 90 degrees.

Routine Work

Before planting, it is a good idea to place a bamboo in the mound in order to liberate ammonia, as if this is not done the mound is apt to get overheated and the plant dies. Syringing has to be done regularly twice a day, the usual amount of water in the mid-growing season being 1 gallon of water to every 3 plants. The walls and paths must also be damped down, especially in hot weather – liquid manure may be used in the afternoon for this purpose if diluted. No laterals must be left on the young plants below the first wire, which should be 18 inches above the tops of the mounds.

Training

The plant may be stopped at the fifth wire, each of them being 1 foot apart, this enables the bottom fruits to swell quicker, and so gives earlier fruiting and marketing.

The rules following this practice are as follows: (1) Do not allow a cucumber to grow on the main stem. (2) Do not allow the lateral to grow further than the second leaf before stopping. (3) Do not take a cucumber and a growth at the same joint; the ideal should be first a cucumber, second a growth where it is stopped, and so on. (4) A good idea is to stop the main laterals at two joints, and the sub-laterals at one joint. (5) Aim at having two fruit-bearing joints on every lateral, and not more than three breaks. (6) Rub out all the male flowers.

All growths must be tied-in to the wires loosely, or growth will be impeded. All young fruits should be kept clear of ties and wires, and should hang cleanly downwards.

Watering

As much harm is done to cucumbers by over-watering as under-watering. If a good deal of old compost has been used, the soil is apt to get sour when over-watered. Moderate waterings are of little use – soak the bed well through twice a week. The water may be at the same temperature as the house.

Shading

When the sun gets bright and scorching in May, shading must be commenced by spraying whitewash over the outside of the glass; towards July this may have to be repeated more heavily, as rains will probably wash the first application off.

Top Dressings

Top dressings and mulchings are essential, and should be given whenever required. ' No-Soil ' Compost should be wheeled into the house at least 12 hours before it is required for use. The first top-dressing may be given 10 days or so after the planting date. It is usual to top-dress again as soon as the white root fibres are seen coming through the surface of the soil. Only a little ' No-Soil ' Compost should be put on every time.

Leaf Cutting

Too often gardeners are fond of cutting away quantities of leaves. No drastic cutting of foliage is really necessary. Cut out any leaves that are turning yellow.

Culture in Frames

Success may be obtained by growing cucumbers in frames, if the following suggestions are carefully carried out. Beds may be made in the frames 2-3 feet deep and a suitable mixture consists of 3 parts sedge peat, and 1 part strawy compost. The peat and compost should be mixed together and allowed to stand for a few days before putting in the frame. The bed will be well trodden down, and a bucketful of earth placed on the bed in a mound at the back of the frame – one mound for each plant, two plants to a 6 feet by 4 feet light are quite sufficient.

Planting should be done a few days afterwards when the soil has warmed up, the same routine being carried out as in the glasshouse. Ventilation will be given if necessary in the daytime to dispel condensed moisture on the frame. During the night, it is advisable to cover the frame lights with sacking. Top dressing will be carried out regularly as previously mentioned for indoor cucumbers, and the growths thinned out, being careful not to overtax the plant with fruit. If the young shoots are pegged down, they themselves will strike and provide fresh vigour to the plant. Regular cutting of the fruits when ready, is also important.

Culture Under Cloches

It is possible to grow cucumbers under cloches or Access frames. Select the variety Conqueror. Raise the plants in the greenhouse as already advised and plant them out in May under the cloches, which should have been erected over a strip of soil to warm it up.

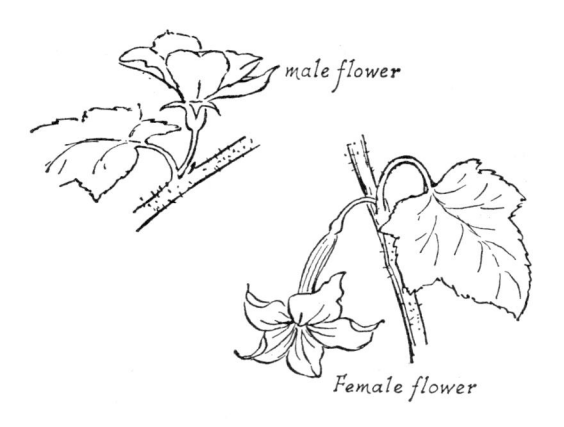

Cucumbers – male and female flowers.

Prepare 'stations' for the cucumbers 3 feet apart by digging out holes 1 foot deep and 1 foot square – fill this hole up with well-rotted compost and tread it down well. Now use the soil excavated mixed with an equal quantity of 'No-Soil' Compost to make a mound 4 inches high and 18 inches wide over each hole. Plant the cucumber in this so that the top of the ball of soil is *just above* the level of the top of the mound.

When the plant has started growing, pinch out the top 1 inch of the main growth to encourage the production of laterals. All you need to do afterwards, is to stop them at one leaf beyond the forming cucumber. A lateral will then form, and this, in its turn, is stopped at one leaf beyond the cucumber, and so on.

These laterals are usually trained or spread out evenly in the cloche. It is possible, however, to allow both the cucumber plants to grow at will and just to cut out laterals when they get too thick.

Pinch off the male blooms from the frame varieties to prevent them pollinating the female blossoms, as this makes the cucumbers bitter. The male flowers, however, are needed in the case of ridge varieties, and these should not be removed, because they ensure a better set and yet no bitterness.

Cut the cucumbers as desired. Never let them become too old. Keep cutting, therefore, when they are of a good size, and the plants will keep cropping. It is possible to get forty good cucumbers from a ridge variety, and about half that number from a good frame type.

The best Ridge variety is Burpless – the fruit isn't as smooth as the frame types, but it is quite delicious. It will grow quite happily under cloches without any special training – but as it is an outdoor variety, the only point of growing the plants under cold glass is to get the fruits earlier.

There is a delicious little cucumber called the Apple cucumber. This is easily grown.

CUCUMBER PESTS AND DISEASES

Red Spider. It is very important to be able to spot this pest immediately. If tackled in its early stages, it can be controlled by cutting out and efficient damping down. Keeping all parts of the house damp is certainly a prevention.

Wood Lice are insidious pests often damaging the plants in the growing season. The only preventive here seems to be trapping – a good trap is a mangold or swede, cut in half and scooped out, and placed upside down on the borders. The wood lice must then be shaken out every day into a bucket of paraffin.

Cucumber Root Fly can cause considerable damage in the propagation stage and in the borders. A very simple control is heavy watering. If this is done, the pest is never a serious matter.

Fungus Troubles
Leaf Spot has in the past caused very serious damage; the

introduction of a disease-resisting variety 'Butchers' has, however, proved a boon to many growers. Prevention – uniform temperature, lime added at each top dressing, thorough cleanliness and not too humid an atmosphere, perfect drainage. Spray with the following wash directly the trouble is first seen – $1\frac{1}{2}$ ounces potassium sulphide, 2 gallons of water. Fourteen pints of water are placed in a bucket, and $1\frac{1}{2}$ ounces of Liver of Sulphur added. Then mix a flour paste, water down with 2 pints of water until as thin as milk. Then boil, stirring all the while, and add to the other bucket containing the Liver of Sulphur and stir.

Mosaic. This disease, noticeable by the mottling and sometimes wrinkling of the leaves, can be transmitted by infected seed, and care should be taken to obtain seed from a nursery free from mosaic. All plants with mosaic should be left until last when trimming, as the sap from the diseased plant may be carried on the knife to a healthy plant. After trimming a mosaic plant, the knife should be sterilised in formaldehyde. No effective cure for this disease has been found.

Root Rot appears at the soil level, the outer tissues turn brown and rot begins, the disease organisms enter the wood and ultimately kill the plant. To control, keep the base of the plant dry; do not water close to the stem. Dust round the base of the plant if attack is suspected, with a dust composed of 10 parts dry slaked lime, 3 parts fine copper sulphate, and 3 parts flowers of sulphur, apply by means of a tin with perforated lid.

Verticillium Wilt appears usually in the lowest leaves, which wilt, turning yellow, the upper leaves then gradually get affected and the whole plant may then become limp and die. The disease is at its worst when the temperature is low, and this is bad in autumn and spring. Increase heat in the greenhouse or frame immediately the disease is first seen. Close the house for 2 hours in the middle of the day. Do not water heavily. Encourage the plant to make new roots by giving 'No-Soil' Compost as a top dressing.

CHAPTER XIV

THE TOMATO STORY

IN all the old books on gardening, the tomato appears under the name Love Apple, but since the earliest days it has been known by the Latin name of *Lycopersicum esculentum,* though the redcurrant tomato which is grown more for curiosity and ornament than for service, because the fruits are so small, is named *Lycopersicum pimpinellifolium.* The Tomato is usually described officially as a tender herb, grown as an annual for its much-prized fruits, either out of doors or under glass. It is, of course, closely related to the potato and a cousin of the deadly nightshade family.

Some authorities say that it was introduced into Great Britain in 1596 when the red-fruited, white-fruited and yellow-fruited types seem to have appeared about the same time. Later on, a variety that crept over the surface of the ground was introduced but, naturally, this never became very popular. Early in the eighteenth century, other types came into the country, such as the cherry-shaped, the pear-shaped, and so on, and today it is still possible to get varieties that bear fruit of various shapes, sizes and colours.

Loudon, in his *Encyclopaedia of Gardening,* published in 1882, states that ' the fruits can be used for sauces and soups, and even in confectionery ', but says nothing about eating tomatoes raw. He does, however, contrast the popularity of this fruit in France and Italy with its unpopularity in Great Britain. He states that near Rome and Naples, tomatoes were grown in fields and that scarcely a dinner was served in which the fruits were not eaten in some way or other.

As late as 1860 and 1870 those who ate tomatoes were considered almost heroes or martyrs, and plants were usually grown in the greenhouse for decorative purposes. Even books published just before the 1914 war almost treated the tomato as a medicine. It was stated, for instance, that the fruits possessed medicinal properties which rendered them desirable as a remedy for the affections of the liver as well as for other organs of the body. Even today, some people regard the taste for tomatoes as one to be acquired, and there are children who regard tomatoes with antipathy.

Those who have read the *Keeper of the Bees,* by Gene Stratton Porter, will remember how the wounded soldier who was due to die was saved by eating tomatoes galore and by drinking the juice. Plenty of sunshine and plenty of tomatoes do seem an excellent combination, don't they? And that is what Gene Stratton Porter's soldier received.

Today, of course, the tomato is used tremendously in sandwiches. In the 1939-45 war people must have blessed this fruit again and again. It makes a grand breakfast when fried. It can be used for soups and stews. It's excellent as a cocktail. The large fruits are first-class when stuffed with cheese or sausage meat, while those who, like myself, do not go in for cocktails, revel in the juice of the tomato with a dash of cayenne pepper in it as an appetiser before a meal. Not that your author ever needs an appetiser, really!

The green tomatoes make excellent chutney; the ripe tomatoes may be bottled and so you can have a supply throughout the winter. It is preferable to skin them first before bottling and you can easily do this if you dip them for a few seconds in boiling water.

The tomato need not be regarded as a tropical plant. It certainly is tender, but the seedsmen have done good work by breeding varieties which are much hardier than those of twenty years ago. There are varieties today that do specially well when grown under continuous cloches: others are first-class out of doors, while some may be grown during the winter months in the greenhouse. There are at least two, Eurocross A and Supercross.

Stockiness the Thing

Everyone agrees that, with the tomato in Great Britain the most important thing is to grow stocky, sturdy, hardy plants and not long, drawn, lanky specimens. Yet, unfortunately, it is so often the tall weedy-looking plants that are sold by the hundred on the coster-barrows and in the shops. If only the public would refuse to buy them and insist on having dwarf, strong, well-developed plants with nice dark-green leaves! — then this would undoubtedly stop this evil trade of poor plants that always give equally poor results.

How Many from How Much?

I have often been asked how many plants one ounce of seed will produce — and the answer is that you can, with luck, get two thousand. It depends, of course, on the variety and on the way the seed has been harvested, and some years ago a grower in Kent, using the variety Hundredfold, was able to produce 40 tons of tomatoes per acre with the aid of cold glass — like cloches — a remarkable feat, considering it is seriously stated in some books that a good yield of tomatoes per acre out of doors is round about 15 tons!

CHAPTER XV

TOMATOES IN THE OPEN

TOMATO plants in the open air, when properly grown and carefully fed, may bear heavier crops for the time they occupy the ground than they do in the greenhouse and there is seldom any difficulty with fertilisation. Every flower seems to set and produces a fruit. Very often the individual fruits are more solid and of a better flavour, though with some varieties it is true to say that the skin may be a little tougher. Get them cropping early and they will continue to produce fruits in profusion until they are cut by autumn frosts.

The tomato prefers a dryish atmosphere and a moderately high temperature coupled, of course, with plenty of sunlight and air. The climate of this country gives no guarantee that these ideal conditions will occur month by month or week by week. It has been said that there are only four good tomato months, June, July, August and September and when, in the north, frosts occur about the third week in September – even this period is reduced by a week or ten days. Much can be done, however, to help matters, if the plants are sturdy, and well forward before they are put out into the open. They should never, however, be planted into cold soil in which the roots cannot work until the temperature rises by several degrees.

They should not be put out so early that there is a chance that the frost will cut them in their prime. They usually love to be in the warmest and most sheltered part of the garden. You can train them with success up a sunny fence or a south wall. In the north, amateurs often use a little spot sheltered on three sides. This is a regular suntrap and can be used with good results.

Better results are always achieved when plants are given plenty of room for development. Overcrowding invariably spells disappointment. You always get better results from fewer plants treated properly; plants put out when the ground is warm;

plants that have had no check; and from plants that begin at once to grow away and to form fruit.

Preparation of the Soil

Taking it by and large, the tomato is not at all particular as to soil. It hates badly-drained land, of course, but, even when well-drained a heavy clay soil is slower to 'warm up' than lighter land. The heavier soils, on the other hand, generally contain more potash than the sandy types and potash is a plant food much beloved by the tomato. The great thing is to fork the ground lightly, and incorporate properly composted vegetable refuse, at the rate of one barrowload to 4 square yards.

Wherever the tomatoes are to be planted, it is always advisable to rake into the soil when preparing the surface tilth, a good organic fertiliser, such as meat and bone meal, hoof and horn meal, or a properly compounded fish manure with a high potash content, at 3 to 4 ounces to the square yard. In the case of the first two fertilisers mentioned, a potassic fertiliser must be used. Wood ashes are best used at 6 to 8 ounces to the square yard. You may use one of the proprietary flue dusts on the market, at about 5 to 6 ounces to the square yard. Ample potash in the ground will help to prevent such troubles as green-back fruits and blotchy ripening.

Raising the Plants

Most people who grow tomatoes out of doors, buy their plants from a good nurseryman, for they haven't the necessary conveniences for raising them. When they do this, they must insist, of course, on having a suitable outdoor variety. Each plant should be showing a flower truss. Always insist on short, sturdy, properly hardened dark-green specimens, which should be planted out some time after the middle of May. Experts have written and said that even in the south it isn't possible to plant out tomatoes until the first week in June, but as we seldom get any frost after about the 16th May, in the south, it is always worth the gamble because the earlier you get the plants in, the better the crop. In the north of course, it is different, and I often found it necessary there, to delay planting until June.

As the actual raising of the plants themselves under glass is the same for outdoor as for indoor planting, look at Chapter XVI for the full details.

A Mild Hotbed

Make this up in a frame about the end of February by putting a 2-foot layer of fresh stable manure* in the bottom. This should have been well ' sweetened ' beforehand, by turning it four times, at intervals of two or three days. Tread the manure down firmly and put 4 to 6 inches of good soil over the top. See that this is levelled and firmed. The seed may then be sown direct into the soil 10 to 14 days later, or if preferred, into shallow boxes filled with Alex ' No-Soil ' Compost.

This can be bought ready to use, direct from the Alex Peat Co., Burnham-on-Sea, Somerset.

The soil used for covering up the horse manure may be the John Innes Seed Compost and then, of course, there is no need to use boxes for raising the plants!

Sowing the Seed

The seed should then be sown in drills drawn out $\frac{1}{4}$ inch deep and 1 inch apart. A little more soil should then be sifted over the top, or a light raking given to cover the seeds. The general aim is to have the surface of the soil parallel to the glass of the light, covering the frame and to see that this is about 6 inches away. It is convenient to sow the seed during the first week in March, and after giving the soil a watering, through the fine rose of a can, the lights should be put in position and covered with sacks or sacking, with the object of keeping the frame warm, and preventing frost from doing any harm. The sacking should be removed as soon as the seeds begin to germinate, but should be replaced each night afterwards in case ' Jack Frost ' should appear.

Pricking Out

Directly the seedlings can be handled, they should be looked over to ensure that they are standing exactly 1 inch apart. The drills, as I said earlier, must be 1 inch apart, and the plants

---

* For those who cannot get horse manure, soil heating may be done by special electrical wires. Consult your local Electricity Board.

the same distance apart in the drills. If the soil gets dry, a little water may be given through a fine rose, but care should be taken to see that the soil never gets in an over-wet condition. The frames can always be ventilated on mild days, but you should guard against cold draughts by raising the sides of the frame on which is, at the time, the windless side, and if the wind should change, that end of the frame should be lowered and the other side raised. It is convenient to use blocks of wood, 2 or 3 inches square for this purpose.

When the plants have made two good leaves, which should be about the beginning of April, you will be wise to thin them out to 2 inches apart either way, and if you like, transplant the thinnings into another frame, or into 3 inch deep boxes of any convenient size filled with John Innes potting compost, or with the 'No-Soil' Compost. These boxes, of course, will have to be kept in a frame or under some glass covering. By the end of April the plants should be growing strongly and sturdily and will again need a further thinning out, this time, to 4 inches apart each way, and again, if necessary, it will be advisable to find further accommodation in boxes or pots for the thinnings. Some amateurs do not bother about the thinnings at all. They purposely sow more seeds than they need, and when they thin out, they use some of the thinnings to fill in any gaps that appear, and then they have just the number of plants they require.

By this time the plants will need a little more head-room. It is therefore advisable to raise the frame light in some way, say, by means of wooden boxes or bricks to hang the sacking over the sides to keep out the draughts. Old sacks are grand for this purpose.

Of course, those who have got a number of frames, can transplant the tomatoes from one to the other and arrange to have more head-room in each case. Incidentally, today it is possible to provide a 'hotbed' by means of electricity. There are firms that supply the correct equipment for ensuring the right type of soil heating, and those who are interested in electrical hot-beds, can always apply for further information to the Electrical Development Department of the local branch of The Electricity Board.

Some people use temporary timber frames. They make these

with boards 6 inches wide and 1 inch thick, cut into the right lengths. They use three of these for the back of the frame and two for the front and they keep them in position by means of laths or cross-pieces nailed on. Then when they want extra height as the plants grow taller, they put another 6-inch wide board at the back and yet another at the front, and they arrange that the end boards are cut in such a manner that they can be fitted into position also.

Planting Out

It should be possible in most districts to set the plants out in the open during the last week of May. In the south, we often used to have a gamble and get the plants out about 15th May, as I have already said, and some have even put them out earlier than this, and got away with it. In the north, it is advisable to wait till the first week of June. At this time, the plants should be sturdy, thick-set and hardy, and about 7 inches high. It is better to wait until the ground is right and the weather clement, than to put the plants out a fortnight earlier in cold, wet, land and when there is a harsh biting wind about.

If the plants are still in boxes, or growing in the soil, in frames, it is necessary to cut the earth into square blocks by passing a sharp knife both ways between the plants and then watering thoroughly. It should be possible then to lift each plant out with its root almost intact and carrying a mass of soil, two days later. Such plants when put out have hardly any check at all. If, of course, by that time the plants have been potted up into 3-inch pots, there is no difficulty in knocking them out, removing the crock and planting the ball of roots when the base of the root system has been purposely disturbed a little. Many prefer to use soil blocks rather than pots and these can be made at home with the correct tool.

Take care to see that the soil round the roots is moist throughout, before putting the plants out into the open. If dry, then they remain so for a long time afterwards and growth will be slow and uncertain. Always water immediately after planting so as to keep the ball of soil moist. This is known as ball watering, but it is advisable to take the precaution of watering the plant when still in the pot, beforehand. Don't plant too deeply, make a hole just deep enough to allow the soil roots to be covered with ½ inch of new soil and see that each plant is trodden in firmly. Plants raised and planted in the way suggested, should begin to grow and bloom right away.

If the growth is confined to a single stem, the plants may be 27 inches apart between the rows and 18 inches apart in the rows. See that the rows run north and south. Where it is desired to do some mechanical cultivation, it may be convenient to have the rows 3 feet apart, to have two rows 27 inches apart, a 3 feet space, another two rows 27 inches apart, and so on.

Supporting the Tomatoes

It is necessary to support the plants in some way. Some people find it possible to have a bamboo or stake to each plant and to tie the stem up to this as it grows. This is an expensive method, not only of material but of labour as well.

Another method is to have posts at the ends of the rows driven at least 2 feet into the ground and with a length of about 5 feet above ground. Straining wires should be arranged at the back of the posts to keep them upright, or another post should be driven in at an angle of 45 degrees on the 'plant' side of the post, and this may then be nailed on to it to give the extra support. A wire should then run from the top of the post, to the post-top at the other end of the row, and it is convenient if a second wire can be run along at ground level. Strings can then be tied between the two wires at each plant, and as the tomato grows, the plants are twisted around the string or, what actually happens in practice, the string is twisted around the plants, and so good support is provided. (For the purpose of estimation, may I say that 1 cwt. of 15 gauge, galvanised wire contains about 1,900 yards.

Another method which is adopted on the score of economy, is to have the top wire and then to tie the base of the string to the bottom of the plant, and the other end of the string to the wire, then as the plant grows it is twisted around the string as before. All kinds of modifications and so-called improvements of this kind have been devised. For instance, I have seen gardeners put up the posts and wires first and then plant two rows of tomatoes, 1 foot away on either side of the wire, 'staggered'.

Strings are then taken from the top wire down to the plants, and as the plants grow they are trained by the twisting method up the strings. It will be seen that in this method the plants bend slightly inward from the left or right, depending on which side of the wire they have been set. You are, however, able to use one wire support for two rows.

Some people prefer to have two stems per plant, and say that this gives them a heavier crop. When this is done, the plants should be set 2 feet, or even 2 feet 6 inches away from one another in the rows and one of the basal shoots should not be rubbed off. The side growth is generally trained perpendicularly and the main growth at an angle of 45 degrees, either up a string or along a bamboo pushed into the ground at this angle.

Cultivation and Training

Regular hoeings should be carried out among the plants to keep down the weeds. Directly any fruit is seen, top dressings of organic matter, such as sedge peat may be given along the rows and around the plants to provide what gardeners call a mulch. All kinds of substances have been used with success, e.g. properly composted vegetable refuse, lawn mowings, spent mushroom beds, old hop manure, finely divided wool shoddy or malt culms.

The side shoots should be pinched off regularly, care being taken not to damage the flower trusses when these shoots are being removed. It is convenient to do this with a sharp thumbnail and forefinger. Never allow side shoots to grow more than 1 inch or so long, except, of course, the bottom one, when you are growing on two stems.

Don't remove any leaves until they are starting to turn yellow. Remember that the foliage manufactures the elaborated sap that sweetens the fruits and causes them to swell. If the leaves seem to be very thick, and it is thought imperative to let in sunlight and air, it is better to cut one or two back to the main stem than to slaughter the foliage by half indiscriminately.

Tie regularly where bamboos or stakes are used. You want a new raffia or 'twist' tie every 6 or 7 inches. Always leave a space for the stem to swell, but do not make the tie so slack that the plants can swing about in every wind. When the plants are growing up strings, it is only necessary to give a little twist around the stem once a week or so, as the plant grows.

Feeding

In addition to the compost and fish manure given to the ground before the plants are set out, it is advisable to feed during the summer with a liquid manure like Farmura, this being a liquid with an ' organic base '. Plants can be given a feed once a fortnight from the time the first trusses are set, until, say, the middle of September.

Tomatoes do not like a very acid soil when growing in the open, so hydrated lime may be given at 3 to 4 ounces to the square yard as a top dressing after the land has been dug and prepared in the winter.

Stopping or Timing

When plants are to be grown entirely in the open, it is necessary to ' time ' or stop the plants during the first week of August. The way to do this is to cut off with a sharp knife the main stem at one leaf above the last truss of flowers, and after this to see that no further side shoots develop. It is inevitable that this stopping should encourage excessive side shoots, and a sharp eye has therefore to be kept on the plants, once they are ' timed '.

Spraying

The great curse of outdoor-tomatoes is the potato blight, which can ruin the tomato crop in the course of a week. It is better to be safe than sorry, and the way to prevent this disease is to spray the plants with Bordeaux Mixture once a fortnight from the end of July onwards. Some people prefer to dust with a copper-lime dust, because this is quicker. If you have an efficient dust gun, it certainly is. In the north it is often necessary to spray once only. There are a number of copper proprietary sprays that give good results; once spraying or dusting starts, it is necessary to wipe the fruits before they are used in the house. Some gardeners use a colloidal copper wash because this doesn't mark the fruit badly.

Picking

Gather the fruits directly they are ripe, and in districts where the birds are a nuisance, it may be necessary to pick when the fruit is half ripe and to continue the ripening under cover. It is heat that helps to ripen tomatoes more than actual sunshine. If, at the end of September, there are still fruits on the 'vines' the trusses should be cut off whole and hung up on wires of the greenhouse or on strings near the window of some room in the house.

It is possible to pick the fruits and wrap them in paper and store them in a box in the spare-room and then use the fruit as it is required. I have had good ripe tomatoes kept in this way until nearly the end of January.

Varieties

It is very difficult to make decisions for readers with regard to varieties, for the old adage 'one man's meat is another man's poison' is almost as true of tomato varieties for growing in the open as of any other garden subject.

I can, however, say that the following varieties have done extremely well in the experimental gardens of the Good Gardeners' Association at Arkley.

Histon Cropper: a dwarf – medium sized fruits.

Easicrop: another dwarf variety.

Outdoor Girl: a heavy cropper.

Ronaclove. ripens even under adverse weather conditions.

CHAPTER XVI

TOMATOES UNDER GLASS

Tomatoes can be grown in many different types of greenhouse, as a visit to any large allotment area near any big city will prove. I have known for instance, tomatoes grow successfully in only 6 inches of soil, placed for the purpose, on the permanent staging of the greenhouse. I have seen them carry heavy crops when growing in pots or boxes placed on the floor or staging of a glass house. In fact, there is a lot to be said for root restriction.

Generally speaking, however, the ideal house for the tomato is what is known as the 'aeroplane' type, where the glass goes down almost to the ground, and where there are ventilators above the door or doors, *and* on either side of the ends of the houses to ensure perfect end-on ventilation. The ideal height would probably be $4\frac{1}{2}$ feet to the gutter and 12 feet to the ridge, though the aeroplane type of house is usually 6 feet to the gutter and 12 feet to the ridge. The plants are grown direct in the border and trained up fillis or string, provided for the purpose.

Tomatoes are usually grown with the idea of covering a whole season – spring and summer. For instance, many gardeners aim to sow the seed in January, to plant out in March and so to start picking at the end of April or early in May and, with care, to keep the plants cropping heavily until the end of September. On the other hand, there are some who like to carry on with their chrysanthemums as late as possible in the greenhouse, or who like to start using their house in the first few months of the year for cucumbers or french beans. In this case, the tomatoes may not be planted, say, until mid-July and the cropping then proceeds until December. Under these late conditions, it is only possible to get about four trusses per plant.

I have found it possible to grow two rows of tomatoes on either side of the main pathway (in pots, of course) in a house of cucumbers. The tomatoes were set out in their pots in February and stopped at two or three trusses. By the time the crop had been picked and the pots whipped out, the cucumbers needed the extra room.

Raising the Plants

Every care must be taken at the 'beginning of the story'. The best seed must be obtained, the compost must be perfect; the boxes must be steamed or dipped in boiling water some time beforehand so that they cannot possibly convey disease or pests. The temperature of the greenhouse should be just right, i.e. about 60 degrees F. while the water used for watering should be absolutely clean and will be round about the same temperature as the house.

The compost used should be the John Innes Seed Compost, or the 'No-Soil' Compost. Stand the soil mixture or compost on the staging of the greenhouse for a few days so that it can warm up before it is used to fill the seed trays.

Use seed trays at least $2\frac{1}{2}$ inches deep; see that they have the necessary drainage holes or slits at the base, cover these with crocks and a little 'rough stuff' and fill the trays in such a manner as to get the same firmness of soil throughout. This ensures that the moisture-holding capacity of the soil is even right through. Always commence firming around the edges and corners, and then level the soil in the centre, and firm. When level, and equally firm right through, there should be a space of $\frac{3}{4}$ inch from the top of the box. Another $\frac{1}{4}$ inch of compost should then be sieved over the top, using a fine meshed sieve, so as to make certain that the top $\frac{1}{2}$ inch in which the seed will go is of the right tilth. This will be lightly firmed in its turn. It is quite simple to make a sieve at home, by fixing a piece of perforated zinc onto a bottomless seed tray.

Space the tomato seeds out individually, making six rows of nine seeds in a row. It is a good idea to have a template of aluminium cut to fit exactly inside the box and bored with holes at exactly the right distance apart. It is then an easy matter to push one seed into each hole. Sieve a further $\frac{1}{2}$ inch fine compost over the top, and lightly firm with firming board. Water through the fine rose of a can, cover the boxes with a sheet of glass and a piece of brown paper or newspaper and stand on the staging of the house at a temperature of 60 degrees F. Turn the glass each morning so that the moisture that has accumulated on the underside gets an opportunity of drying out.

Remove the glass as soon as the seedlings appear, but leave the paper on for a day or two. Then expose the seedlings to full light. Germination should take place within one week, and seeds that do not grow in that time, generally produce useless plants. Keep the atmosphere of the house on the damp side, so syringe the pathways and walls once or twice a day.

If a dull, somewhat coolish period prevails at this time of the year, it may be necessary to keep the seedlings on the dry side. The whole point is that the baby plants should not be over- or under-watered. It is no use, therefore, watering if the soil is sufficiently moist and the plants do not need it. It is largely a question of evaporation. When the house is dry and the weather warm, the leaves of the plants give off a lot of moisture and then the roots need more to take in.

Partial Soil Sterilisation

Gardeners always talk about soil sterilisation, whereas, actually, of course, one should really refer to partial sterilisation. The object of such sterilisation is to kill all diseases and pests and render the weed seeds inactive. The temperature of the soil should be raised to between 180 and 210 degrees F. and should be kept at that temperature for about fifteen minutes, and then allowed to cool.

1. *Electricity*

It is possible for a gardener to sterilise soil by electricity, and those who light or heat their house electrically can apply to the Regional Offices of The Electricity Board who will give them full details as to the cost of a soil sterilising outfit.

2. *The Bucket Method*

A very simple way of sterilising a small quantity of soil is to fill a bucket with the earth to be treated and hang it from a crossbar put over a copper of boiling water. A lift of some sort should be fitted to the bucket and a potato the size of an egg should be buried in the soil 1 inch down. The bucket should be suspended so that the water reaches to within 1 inch of the top and heat should be applied to the water so that it constantly boils, until the potato is cooked. This is somewhat of a rule-of-thumb method, but it does work. Those whose wives still boil their clothes in a copper, will find it a useful method of using up the soap-sud water towards the end of a 'washing morning'!

3. *Another Bucket Method*

Another method of using a gas, or other copper, is to pour two gallons of water into the bottom and then to put a perforated wooden or steel framework, 2 inches above the water level, which will allow the steam to penetrate. On to this framework should be stood a bucket filled with the soil it is desired to sterilise. The bucket should be perforated all over with holes $\frac{1}{8}$ inch in diameter and 3 inches apart. The heat should be applied to the water and it should be possible to cause it to boil in ten minutes or so and thus to cause the soil in the bucket to read a temperature of 210 degrees F. in half an hour. Ten minutes after this the soil should be sterilised and may be tipped out and used. A further charge may then be put in and the operation repeated. The lid of the copper should always be kept in position to prevent the steam from escaping.

Potting Up

The seedlings may be allowed to go on growing in the boxes or seed trays until two true leaves have developed, for by then they will have started a really good root system. They should be potted up therefore as early as possible into 3 inch pots or soil blocks, the compost on this occasion being that known as the John Innes Potting Compost, or if in pots, the 'No-Soil' Potting Compost.

Put this compost into the house for a day or two to warm up, so that it is at the same temperature as the soil in the seed trays, where the little tomatoes are growing. See that the pots are absolutely clean. If they are old, wash them and scrub them well in plenty of hot water and then set them in the sunshine to dry. Crock the holes at the bottom and put a little rough material like old leaves, bits of turf, over the crock. Hold the seedling in position in the centre of the pot with one hand, and fill the pot up with the compost with the other. Remember that you must only handle the leaves and never grip the stem. When the pot is full of the compost you can use both hands for firming the soil into the pot without actually touching the seedling. Apply pressure to the soil just inside the rim of the pot, tapping slightly on the bench. Then add a little more compost if necessary, tap and firm again until the soil is level to within ¼ inch of the top of the pot. This leaves just the right amount of room for watering.

When you have finished the job, the plant should be right in the middle of the pot. The seed leaves should be resting on the soil which should be absolutely level. The compost in the pots should be moderately firm and it should not be possible to see any finger or thumb depressions on the surface of the soil. If you are a novice at this job, it is always worth while taking time. Practice makes perfect. When you become really good at this work, you will be able to pot up over 100 in half an hour!

Stand the pots on the staging of the greenhouse, touching one another, and then give them a good watering through the fine rose of a can. It has always been thought necessary to have the water at the same temperature as the house, but experiments are proceeding that seem to show that colder water does no harm. Keep the temperature of the house, if possible, at 65 degrees F. at night time and allow the house to rise to 70 degrees F. during the day. This always helps to overcome the disturbance the plants receive during potting. At the same time, carry out efficient syringing of the walls and paths, so as to charge the house with moisture. In a week's time, the temperature may be reduced and so may the syringings.

The plants should start to grow quite quickly and when it is seen that growth is starting, ventilation should be given during the middle of the day, starting with half hour then one hour and then, as the plants continue to grow, ventilation may be given from, say, 10 a.m. until 3.30 p.m. The great thing is to keep the plants short jointed and not to allow them to become long and leggy. To ensure this, space the plants out with 3 inches between them, after they have been in the house a fortnight or three weeks. Try to keep the pots on the staging of the house so that they are near the light all the time. If you have to stand the pots on the floor of the house, sift plenty of sand or fine ashes over the soil first to discourage the plants rooting through the drainage hole into the soil below.

The new plastic pots are first-class at this stage. Some growers prefer to plant the baby tomatoes in trays 3 inches apart, and they grow them on in these receptacles until they are about 8 inches high. It is possible then to use a long-bladed knife and to cut through the compost and matted roots so as to leave a nice square of soil to each plant. If this is done a week before planting, the plants appreciate it tremendously.

As I have said on another page, it pays to keep a sharp lookout during this stage for the rogues as they are called. Some plants grow more like ferns, or are 'feather headed'; some are dwarfed and the leaves seem to form a little rosette. Some seem to grow more like little fir trees. All these abnormal-looking plants should be removed immediately they are seen. Gardeners often call these rogues 'Jacks' or 'Christmas Trees'.

Preparing the Border

It usually takes two months from the time of sowing for the plants to be ready to put out. Directly therefore, the previous crop in a tomato house has been harvested, the ground should be prepared by bastard trenching as it is sometimes called.

During the digging, properly composted vegetable waste will be incorporated at one 2-gallon bucketful to the square yard. In addition, if tomatoes have been grown in the same ground for a *great* many years and sufficient compost has not been given each season, it is advisable to see that the physical condition of the soil is perfect by digging in straw put in *vertically* (please note that). The straws act as air tubes and aerate the lower soil, the bacteria are kept working, and watering is assisted.

Naturally, this putting in of layers of straw upright in the trench, takes longer than ordinary digging, but the results are so much better that it is worth it. Don't use straw that has been baled, because during the baling the air tubes are squashed. The straw is always used in addition to compost manure and not instead of it, and only in cases where the soil in tomato houses has been used for a great number of years for tomato growing.*

---

* Lately I have been growing the tomatoes in long narrow plastic bags filled with Alex 'No-Soil' compost and thus no digging of the border has to be done.

While doing this digging, it is necessary to flood the trenches to get the subsoil thoroughly wet. I have heard it said that if it is not made too wet beforehand, then it never will be wet. The time at which flooding should take place, naturally, depends on the surface soil and the subsoil. Generally speaking, a heavy clay soil doesn't require much water, whereas a light sandy soil needs a lot.

The aim should be to give about 25 gallons to 500 square yards. The flooding should always be done after the straw has been laid in position, because it does require wetting.

It is usually only necessary to add lime to heavy soils in order to improve their physical condition. Experiments, however, do seem to show that in normal cases under glass, lime is not necessary because tomatoes prefer a slightly acid soil. Sedge peat is very useful and is used to improve the physical condition, and when used, is generally applied at the rate of 5 bales to 300 square yards. In very sandy soils, sedge peat is damped first and this helps to hold the moisture. It is normally only used on heavy clays, however, for the purpose of improving its workability.

As to fertilisers, these should always be as far as possible, organic in character. A fish fertiliser is usually used at the rate of $\frac{1}{4}$ lb. per square yard – one with a 10 per cent potash content. In addition, finely divided wood ashes can be 'foods' given at 2 lb. per square yard. These should be applied after all the digging has been done and be pricked into the top 3 or 4 inches with a fork. It is always advisable to get the fertilisers into the soil about three weeks before planting, though the gardener can take an intercrop of winter lettuces in between the tomatoes if the manures are applied in November, so that the lettuces can be planted during the second week of December.

Planting

Planting should take place when the plants are 6 to 8 inches high with a really good root system. Many gardeners like to plant them when the first truss is visible. If the house is heated, the heat should be 'put on' a fortnight before planting, so that the temperature of the soil is not less than 58 degrees F. If you plant when the soil temperature is lower than this, the roots invariably die and then fungus diseases will attack them, and even though the plant may not die altogether, its cropping capacity will be lessened. Another advantage, I must mention, is that there is a bacillus that will not attack the tomato if the soil is at a temperature of 58 degrees F. or over.

It is usual to plant in rows across the house, giving the plants 12 inches apart in the rows; the second row is then put 18 inches away and the third row 27 inches away. Thus, you have two rows, 18 inches apart, then a 27 inch space, and the advantage is that workers can walk up the 27-inch alleyway and the soil only gets trodden down in the wide row and never in the 18 inch space. A main pathway, is of course, run down the centre of the house.

The plant is removed from the pot by turning it upside down, and then putting the stem in between the second and third fingers of the left hand, the rim of the pot is tapped on something solid and this frees the ball of roots and the soil. The pot can then easily be removed with the right hand and laid on the ground. The ball of roots must be thoroughly wet before planting. Some gardeners prefer to put the plant pot and all, in the ground for a day or two and then to knock the plant out of the pot afterwards, when the soil in the pot has got acclimatised to the soil in the house. The hole for the reception of the ball of soil, or the pot, is usually made with a dibber of about the same size, or where this is not available, with a trowel.

Never plant unless the soil is warm enough. Never pull loose soil around the collar of a plant because if there are any wireworms in the house at all, this will give them an opportunity of working through. If the ball of soil is exposed and hard, wireworms find some difficulty in attacking. Plant so that the top of the ball is *just below the level** of the soil, and so that the top of the tomato appears as if it had been planted in the middle of a shallow saucer.

In the case of the modern soil block, there is of course, no knocking out of pots to do. The block holding the plant is set in the ground firmly – a hole having been made for its reception with a trowel.

* While with cucumbers it is always just above.

After Planting

See that the plants are watered two or three days after planting and again seven days later. Do this with a fine rose attached to a watering can. After this, it shouldn't be necessary to water the plants for some considerable time – probably not till the flowers of the second truss are opening, i.e. about six weeks. If you water too much, there is a tendency for the plants to make too much foliage and not to fruit as they should. Keep the temperature of the house at about 60 degrees F. at night time, and on bright mornings, water the pathways through the fine rose of a can and damp the hot-water pipes at the same time.

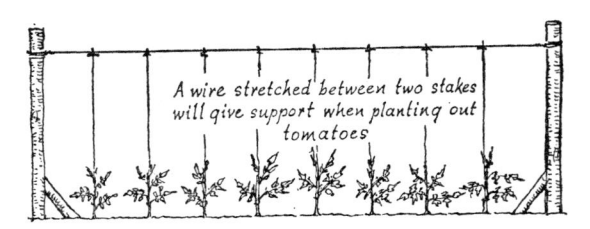

A wire stretched between two stakes will give support when planting out tomatoes

Training Tomato plants out of doors.

Supporting the Plants

It will be necessary to support the plants in some way. The old-fashioned method was to give each plant a good bamboo, but unfortunately (a) bamboos are expensive and (b) they provide hibernating quarters for red spiders, thus becoming a source of infection the next year. The cheapest method, however, and the one most commonly used, is to run a length of wire, say, 14 gauge, at soil level, anchoring it tightly at both ends, and keeping it at soil level by using similar wire, bent to form hairpins, 2 feet long, and pushing these into the ground every 10 feet. Another wire of similar gauge is then fixed overhead at the top of the house, and 4-ply tomato string or fillis is then tied between the two wires. These 'anchor' and overhead wires should, of course, be fixed to coincide with the rows of plants and the strings will be tied in such a way that there is one to each plant.

Some gardeners try to save by not having the wire at

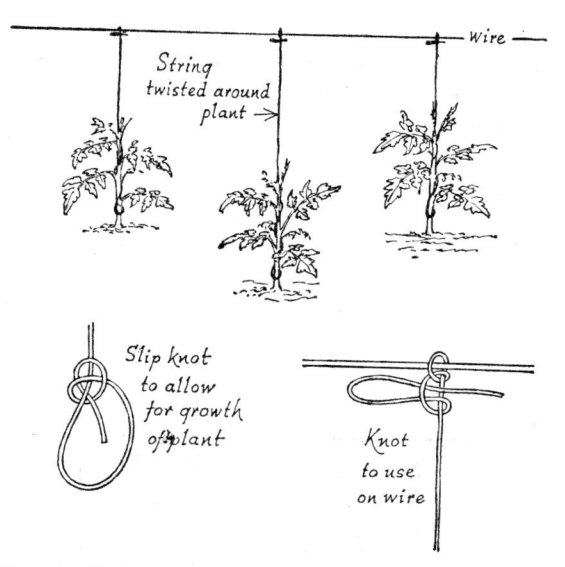

How the Tomato plants are tied and grown up strings.

Tomato growing.

soil level and then they tie fillis from the top wire to the base of each plant. The result is that the plants are often damaged during the season, for while working they may be pulled up.

At the end of the season it is advisable to burn the string to prevent an infection of Botrytis being 'carried over'. It is always convenient to tie the strings to the wires with slip knots that can easily be untied at the end of the season. The plants are not actually tied up to the string, but as they grow the string is twisted around them in a spiral fashion. It is quite an easy job to do.

Training and Management

The training consists largely of removing the side shoots which will be found growing in the axils of the leaves. If side shooting is done in the early morning, the shoots snap out easily when given a sharp sideways pull. The great object is to leave no stump at their base which may become diseased. Many gardeners prefer to dis-shoot by using a knife blade and this is a very good method. If a knife blade is used, great care must be taken to see that it is never placed in a pocket where there is tobacco dust, or virus diseases will be spread. Some have found it necessary to sterilise the knife blade in a Formalin solution after treating any plants which look at all 'under the weather'.

Hand twisting on the other hand, is always better done in the afternoon when the stems are more flaccid. If by any chance, the tip or growing point of a plant becomes injured, a good gardener will allow a side shoot to develop which can be trained up in its place.

Some gardeners like to leave four or five side shoots on a plant when it is first put into the ground, and they say this helps it to develop more quickly. They then remove the side growths when they are 6 to 7 inches long. If you find that the root system seems to be weakening owing to over-cropping, you can overcome this by leaving some of the side shoots to grow 7 inches long or so, thus encouraging further root development.

Don't defoliate at all while the plants are green and healthy.

Cut off the bottom leaves after they have turned yellow, which is usually when about five trusses have set. The scheme generally advocated, is to cut off all the leaves between the soil level and the bottom truss, when this is starting to ripen. A fortnight later, remove all the leaves up to the next truss and the simplest way of doing this is to hold the leaf stalk 2 inches from the main stem and then give a sharp pull upwards. The leaf comes away naturally, leaving no awkward wound. When this cannot be done, the sharp blade of a knife is necessary to cut the base of the leaf stem off close to the main stem.

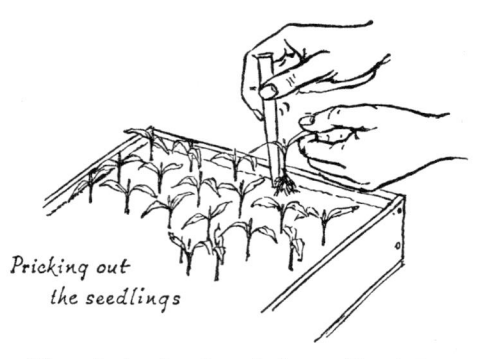

Pricking out the seedlings

There is the drawing of the seedling being potted-up on another page.

Stopping or Timing

The pinching out, or cutting out of the growing point of a tomato plant is generally called stopping or timing. This is often done at the fourth or fifth truss. Experiments have shown, however, that there is no advantage in this method unless, of course, the plants have got to the top of a low house and there is no room for them to go further. Do not stop, therefore, until there is no further head-room for the plant, and even if it has reached its limit, see if you cannot train it along an overhead wire and so form an archway of growth, say over the path.

Pollen and Fertilisation

Syringing the plants undoubtedly helps to distribute pollen and so ensures perfect fertilisation. This work should be done early in the day so as to ensure that the plants are nice and dry before the house is closed down at night time. Some gardeners like to shut the house for two hours after syringing, because they say that if the temperature is increased, the setting of the fruit is assisted. A difficulty often occurs when the plants have got to the top of the house, because the flowers there, being more exposed to the sun, get dried up.

This is another reason why it is a good plan to allow side shoots to develop at the tip of the plant, for the leaves thus formed give greater shade to the flowers and so assist in the process of fertilisation. Furthermore, this extra foliage helps to keep the fruits from becoming too hard. Some gardeners jar the wires of a house, with the object of causing the pollen to fly out and thus they help with the operation of pollination.

Water and Mulches

It is very difficult indeed to give advice about watering. If too little is given, the plants may suffer, and if too much, then root action may stop. The great thing is to prepare the soil thoroughly with adequate water in the winter when the border is being prepared. Naturally, if soils are very well drained, it is seldom that over-watering is ever experienced. It is only on badly drained land that it may occur. Another trouble that is seldom realised is that the moment you water, the soil temperature falls, and this, of course, is a particularly difficult problem during the months of April and May, when it is difficult to keep the ' heat ' up.

When watering, apply the water on the surface of the ground so as not to splash, because if moisture does splash on the fruits then diseases may occur. Once the middle of June is over, it is usually necessary to water once a week, or on very dry soils, twice a week. If because a crust seems to form on the surface of the ground the water can't get through, break it up first with a fork by plunging this into the ground every 3 feet or so and moving it backwards and forwards.

Mulching, i.e. top dressings of sedge peat, hop manure, plain straw, etc. may be done to a depth of 3 to 4 inches. Some gardeners prefer to use wheat straw all over the surface of the soil to a depth of 8 or 9 inches, and this has given very good results. Remember, if some kind of dung is used it should be spread out in the open first of all to cool it and prevent fermentation. You must not put fresh dung into a house, for it will give off ammonia and damage the plants. Mulches not only help to keep the moisture down below, but they stop the soil splashing on the fruits when watering.

Ventilation

A good gardener is one who knows how to ventilate his house properly. In the early part of the year, the wind should never be allowed to blow on to the plants and so the ventilators should only be opened on the lee side. If the plants seem to flag a bit, then it is always possible to syringe them over, rather than to try to put on too much air. Of course, when it comes to the middle of June, it should be possible to give plenty of ventilation in the day-time if the weather is hot. Indeed, it is often advisable in mid-summer to leave some of the ventilation open at night time as well.

In addition during the hot weather, the doors at the end of the house should be left open if there isn't a strong wind. Too much wind tends to dry out the border and causes the leaves to transpire over much. It is always possible to open the doors at the north end of the house and not at both ends.

Do not be tempted to cut off all the heat from June onwards, and then try to keep up the temperature by closing the ventilators early. The result of this particular system, is that invariably a bad attack of *Cladosporium fulvum,* the tomato mould, is experienced. Keep a little warmth on and you ensure a buoyant atmosphere plus a movement of air. Remember that your ventilators are there to help you prevent a rapid rise of temperature, and not to cool the air that is already in the house (please read this sentence carefully). It is the sudden cooling of the air which causes moisture to condense, not only on the glass but on the plants and thus encourages the dreaded fungus disease.

The general aim should be to keep the night temperature of a tomato house at about 60 degrees F. and, of course, to allow the temperature to rise much higher than this during the day.

Summer Manuring

The first feeding is normally given after the second truss has set and should consist of a fish manure with a high potash content, waiting another three weeks before applying a further similar dressing.

When the houses are quite small, fine wood ashes may be used in addition, at ½ lb. to the square yard. Many gardeners are finding that one of the modern proprietary liquid manures, like Farmura, provides the desired results. These liquid feeds will be given when the watering is due, once a fortnight. The small gardener will, of course, put the right quantity of tomato Liquinure into his can from the bottle and water it on. The general plan under the liquid manure method will be to feed once a fortnight from the time the second truss has set onwards.

Dis-shooting tomato plant

N.B. – Do not try to feed a plant that has not got adequate roots to absorb it. When the roots systems are bad, the only way to help matters is to give a good mulching of sedge peat to a depth of, say 3 inches all over the soil and thus encourage the plants to root higher up. When the new roots have formed, feeding may recommence.

Growing in Pots or Boxes

Sometimes for one reason or another, it is not convenient to grow tomatoes in the border of the house, and then they have to be grown in pots or boxes on the staging. The preliminary work, raising the plants and so on, is the same and all that has to be done is to set the plants out into the large pots, 8 or 10 inches or whatever they may be, or into the boxes like orange boxes, provided for the purpose. When transferring the plants, the ball of soil in the smaller pot should be kept intact and a hole of sufficient size dug out of the soil in the larger pot with a trowel.

When first planted, the 10 inch pots or large boxes should be filled with compost (John Innes Compost No. 2 or 'No-Soil' Potting Compost) to within 4 inches of the top, to allow top dressings to be added later. The plants should be pressed in firmly. Water should be given sparingly in the early stages, as it is not desired to encourage soft and rapid growth. Once,

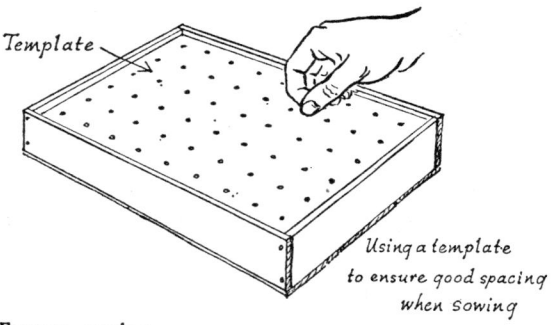

Tomato sowing.

Using a template to ensure good spacing when sowing

Young seedlings growing well with plenty of space for growth

however, the first truss has set, regular watering will be given, usually twice a week.

Dis-shoot the plants as advised for those growing in the border, and feed from the time the second truss has set, each week, using the Liquinure. Stop the plants when they get to the top of the space allotted and train them by means of wires and string as already suggested. When several clusters of fruit have set, a top dressing will be necessary. This should consist of 2 inches of John Innes Potting Compost No. 2 or the 'No-Soil' Potting Compost, and six weeks afterwards give another top dressing 1 inch deep. After each operation a good watering is necessary. As the weather gets warmer the plants will need watering more often, until by mid-June it will be necessary to water every day.

A Late Crop
Some people specialise in growing a crop of late tomatoes in pots or boxes, and to do this they sow seeds in boxes at the end of May to obtain the right size plants to pot-up during the first week of July. They usually grow the plants on during the summer out of doors, taking care to prevent them being attacked by the potato blight, by spraying the plants once a fortnight, from the third week of July onwards, with a good Bordeaux Mixture or other Copper wash. They give a liquid manure feed from mid-August onwards and then lift the pots into the house about the third week of September and so ensure having tomatoes to pick until mid-December. The tip is to keep the house almost at the same temperature as that outside for the first two weeks after housing the plants and then to grow them on, so that the highest temperature is not more than about 50 degrees F.

Picking
It should be possible to pick, eighteen weeks after seed sowing, though with the very early sowings, it may be twenty-two weeks. For home consumption, it is always better to gather the fruit when the skin is red all over, and many people suggest that tomatoes have their highest flavour if picked in the early evening. Always pick so that the calyx remains attached to the fruits, so take hold of the tomato, lift it upwards slightly, and it should detach quite easily from its little footstalk. Some people like to keep the tomatoes in a cool pantry for at least 24 hours before using them, as they say they improve under this method.

When the Crop is Over
When the whole crop has been picked the tomato plants, or haulm as it is called, can be taken out and put onto the compost heap. It is curious, but true, that the tomatoes grown on tomato haulm compost, invariably crop very heavily indeed. The

strings will be burnt and the house will be ready to fumigate and wash down. To work out the amount of fumigation material required, it is necessary to multiply the length of the house by its width by its average height, and this will give the number of cubic feet. The proprietary substance to be used for fumigation will have on the tin or container the number of ounces that should be used per 1,000 cubic feet. See that the ventilators are closed, block up any holes there may be with newspaper made sodden with water, sprinkle the fumigating chemical along the paths in the evening, and close down for the night.

It is possible to buy what are often called Smoke Bombs – these are lit in the evening after the doors and ventilators are closed, and the fumes given off kill the insect pests.

The following morning, open the house up and let out the gas, and then wash down the woodwork of the house with hot soapy water. Try to use a little carbolic disinfectant in the water if possible, and see that the corners are well scrubbed.

Other Necessary Hygienic Operations

Many of the virus diseases that attack tomatoes are transmitted from the hands of workers. Smokers, before handling tomatoes should always wash their hands in a strong disinfectant, for the American tobacco plant viruses, which are not killed when the tobacco leaf is ' cured ', are undoubtedly one of the worst causes of tomato troubles. Never smoke, therefore, when working with tomatoes, and never let nicotine-stained fingers touch the plants. Better still, don't smoke at all!

See that the pots and boxes for tomatoes are clean. Sterilise them by steaming them or pouring boiling water over them. Chemical sterilisation can be achieved by placing the pots or boxes in a tank containing a 2 per cent solution of formaldehyde for forty-eight hours. Remove the pots and boxes, drain them, and do not use them until all traces of Formalin smell has disappeared. Scrub the staging of the greenhouse or frame with formaldehyde, so as they say, to ' make absolutely certain '.

The Compost or Soil Mixture

Give the plants the right start by preparing what may be called a scientific compost devised by the John Innes Horticultural Institution or use the Alex 'No-Soil' compost. The J.I., compost can be made up with really good loam, plus good sedge peat, and coarse sand. The particles of the peat should grade evenly from $\frac{1}{8}$ inch to $\frac{3}{8}$ inch in size. The peat moss litter used by poultry keepers is unsuitable for the purpose. The sand should be clean and sharp and free from silt, powdered shells and organic matter. To get the best results the material should be sterilised separately, but this especially applies to the soil, Good horticultural peat and sharp sand seldom need sterilising.

>   2 parts by bulk good soil (sterilised)
>   1 part by bulk sedge peat
>   1 part by bulk coarse sand

Add to this compost $1\frac{1}{2}$ ounces of superphosphate and $\frac{3}{4}$ ounce of ground chalk per bushel, or two pounds of superphosphate and 1 pound of ground chalk per cubic yard.

If the tomatoes are to be potted up into 3-inch pots later, the soil mixture used should be as follows:

>   7 parts by bulk good soil (sterilised)
>   3 parts by bulk sedge peat
>   2 parts by bulk coarse sand

If the loam is sandy and light, a slight modification is possible and the formula should then be:

>   8 parts by bulk sandy soil
> $2\frac{1}{2}$ parts by bulk sedge peat
> $1\frac{1}{2}$ parts by bulk coarse sand

To this potting compost should be added $\frac{1}{4}$ lb. John Innes base and $\frac{3}{4}$ ounce of ground chalk per bushel, or 5 lb. John Innes base and 1 lb. ground chalk per cubic yard.

The formula for John Innes base is:

2 parts hoof and horn, $\frac{1}{8}$ inch grist (13 per cent nitrogen)
2 parts superphosphate of lime (16 per cent phosphoric acid)
1 part sulphate of potash (48 per cent pure potash)
>   All by weight

If the best results are to be achieved, the quantities of the fertilisers given should be exact. Don't just guess. Try and measure carefully. If the soil used tends to be wet, spread it out to dry and get it down really fine, if possible passing it through a ⅜-inch sieve. Break the peat up by rubbing it through a sieve of the same size. Sprinkle it with water afterwards through the fine rose of a can. Spread the soil out on the bench or floor 2 to 3 inches deep, and then spread the peat out on top, and the sand on top of that. You will have no difficulty in mixing the three evenly together by turning them over and over again with a clean spade.

If you propose to mix the two composts at the same time so that the potting compost is ready for later use, then it is quite a good plan to mix red brick rubble dust in with the potting compost to add colour, and this will prevent confusion.

What is a Bushel of Soil?

A bushel equals 2,200 cubic inches. A box 22 inches long, 10 inches wide and 10 inches deep, holds exactly 1 bushel of soil.

How Much to Make Up?

Readers may want to know how much compost to make up and the following figures should help :

> 1 bushel of compost is sufficient for 100 plants in 3-inch pots
> or 45 plants in 4½-inch pots
> or 9 seed trays, 14 inches by 8½ inches by 2 inches
> or 6 seed trays, 14 inches by 8½ inches by 3 inches

If you are potting-on from small pots :

> 1 bushel of compost is sufficient for potting-on :
> 50 plants from 3-inch pots to 4-inch pots
> 25 plants from 3-inch pots to 6-inch pots

Those who are anxious not to use any artificial fertilisers at all, may use steamed bone flour instead of the Superphosphate and wood ashes instead of the Sulphate of Potash – using twice the quantities in each case.

The No-Soil Composts

The Compost contains no loam or soil. A specially selected and processed Peat has been produced, to do the work of both loam and peat in this Compost, more efficiently than the loam and peat together, in a traditional Compost. The processed peat is mixed with plant nutrients and a special type of sand. The John Innes Compost is likely to give inferior results, if the loam used in it is not a really good one.

Outstanding Advantages

No-Soil Composts have many outstanding advantages over John Innes and similar Composts. They are easier to use and store and they provide a standard growing medium, which has the same constant quality wherever it is bought. The problem of unsatisfactory Compost due to a sub-standard loam is eliminated. Alex ' No-Soil ' Composts have better aeration, moisture holding, and plant food retention and release properties. A better root action is obtained and the same size pot will carry a slightly larger plant. No sterilisation is necessary.

Instructions for Use

The Seedling Compost is ideal for raising seeds. Water should be added at the rate of 10 pints per bushel, or $1\frac{1}{4}$ pints per gallon of the Seedling Compost, and mixed very thoroughly. Fill the seed tray evenly and tamp down to get a level surface. Sow the seed and cover the Seedling Compost of the same thickness as the size of the seed. Very small seeds should be pressed into the compost, no further covering being necessary. If the seed tray is covered with glass or plastic, remember to turn the covering daily and wipe off condensation. Do NOT allow the plastic covering to touch the surface of the compost or the germinating seedling. Keep the compost moist but not waterlogged; watering, when necessary, should be done with a fine mist spray in the early stages and subsequently, a fine rose. If the seed tray dries out by mistake, place the tray in 2 inches of water and allow to soak until thoroughly moist.

Making Up Potting Compost

No. 1. Add 11 ounces Potting Base per bushel of Seedling Compost
No. 2. Add 22 ounces Potting Base per bushel of Seedling Compost
No. 3. Add 33 ounces Potting Base per bushel of Seedling Compost

Note – For small quantities remember 1 bushel equals 8 gallons. To convert 1 pint Seedling Compost to Potting Compost No. 1, add 3 level teaspoonsful of Potting Base and then half a teacup of water.

Mix the base and compost together very thoroughly, and then add 10 pints of water per bushel and mix thoroughly again.

Watering

Keep the Alex Compost more moist than John Innes Compost, this gives the best results and reduces the total amount of watering necessary. If the Composts are allowed to dry out by mistake, allow the pots to stand in a deep saucer or bowl of water until thoroughly moist.

CHAPTER XVII

TOMATOES UNDER GANWICKS OR CLOCHES

THE growing of tomatoes completely in the open as described in the previous chapter, may be considered by some a gamble. In 1958 for instance, a notoriously wet year, few people gathered more than two pounds or so per plant (and many picked no sound tomatoes at all) whereas under Cloches, the average throughout the country was $6\frac{1}{2}$ lb. per plant. If this can happen in one of the worst years ever known, it will be seen that Cloches can be ideal for tomato production.

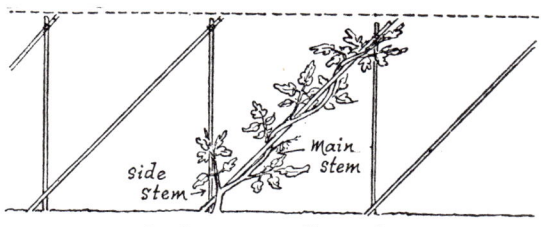

Tomatoes under glass Ganwicks.

What are Ganwicks?

The modern 'continuous cloches' must never be confused with the old-fashioned bell jar which was originally called the cloche by the French. Ganwicks are a type of cloche but very closely related to a frame; they are not in themselves complete entities, each unit, or 2 foot section, interlocking with its neighbours to form a continuous whole. The panes of glass slide into this framework which holds them firmly but without tension, and these panes remain easily removable for quick and complete access to the crop, either from the top or side.

Ganwicks are obtainable in three heights, 12", 18" and 24",

but it is only the last two which can be of any real use for tomatoes. The 24″ Ganwick is, of course, the first choice, being a truly roomy structure; it is 24 inches high (hence its name) by 33 inches wide and the 2-foot sections can be linked together to form a row of any required length. If the plants are planted in trenches, according to the method described on p. 34 and diagonal staking is also practised (see p. 163), it is possible to keep the plants covered with these large Ganwicks for almost the whole of the season.

The 18″ model, either as a 'Single' or a 'Double' is, however, successfully used for tomatoes all over the country. The meaning of the terms 'Single' or 'Double' Ganwick will be easily understood by referring to the diagram on p. 202. A 'Single' model (of whatever height) is one where a single span is used to support 2 side panes and 1 top pane, each section being linked to its neighbours to form a row of any length but never more than one span in width. A 'Double' model means that two spans have been linked together to give nearly double the width. 'Doubles' are a great saving in glass for, whereas 3 panes are required to glaze a section of 'Single' Ganwick, only 4 panes are need for a 'Double', and it is this, coupled with the added advantage of saving much space that would otherwise be wasted in pathways, that has given Ganwick Doubles their immense popularity.

A Double 18″ Ganwick has a width of 45 inches and, with this model, two rows of tomatoes should be planted side by side at 22 inches apart (i.e. down the centre of each span). It is not possible to give the plants extra height by setting them in a trench when using Double 18s, as the middle feet of the spans must be on firm and level ground, or the top panes will not sit snugly in position. The easiest method is therefore to allow the plants to grow unsupported until they reach a height of 18 inches, then remove all the top panes and either stake the plants or string them to wires as described on p. 163. The Single 18″ Ganwick is 24 inches wide and can be used over a trench if preferred. It is a simple matter to carry out the potting on a little board or table put near the greenhouse.

Good Seed

Always get the best seed from a reliable source. There are strains within varieties and, unfortunately, a name today is not necessarily any guarantee. It is the special seedsman's strain, of that particular variety, which does make all the difference. Always purchase seed, therefore, from a first-class seedsman, whose reputation is at stake.

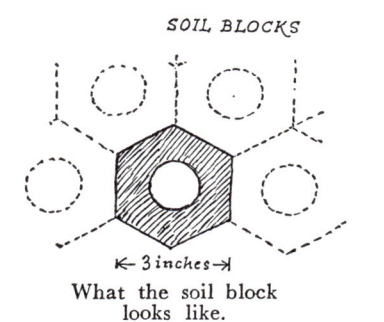

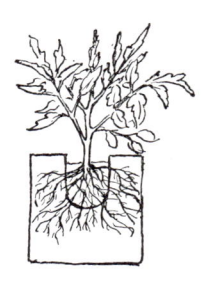

SOIL BLOCKS

|← 3 inches →|

What the soil block looks like.

A Tomato plant in a soil block.

Sowing Seeds and Raising Plants

The seeds can be sown in the greenhouse as advised on p. 168. Those who have no greenhouses had better buy in plants – but if it is desired to grow your own seedlings – then sow the seeds in shallow drills 6 inches apart under 2 or 3 Ganwicks in April and when the plants are seen – thin the seedlings out to 3 inches apart. Later thin to 6 inches apart, and transplant the thinnings on this occasion to new rows. When the plants are 6 inches high they may be planted out in the normal way.

Soil Block Making

For making the Soil Blocks one can always use the John Innes Potting Compost No. 1, which one can buy in for the purpose – or the Alex 'No-Soil' Compost if it is made sufficiently moist. Some gardeners add a little sterilised soil to the normal no-soil compost, as they say that the blocks remain in a better condition when this is done.

When the third rough leaf has developed, their is no difficulty in transplanting the seedlings into the compressed soil pots made with the Alex Soil Block Maker. A plan-tool is plunged several times in a pile of compost until the cup is packed tightly with soil, a foot lever compresses the soil, and makes a central hole and the completed pot is 'ejected' by depressing a handle.

N.B. – Remember
1. It takes about eight weeks from the time of sowing to produce a tomato plant fit to put out in its cropping position.
2. Always take the trouble to mix up the right compost, unless you use the Alex 'No-Soil' Compost.
3. Sterilise any soil used.
4. Handle seedlings with great care.
5. Never expose the plants (or transplant them) during cold, windy weather.
6. Use reliable, healthy seed.
7. Give protection to plants during excessive frost or excessive sunshine in the earlier part of the season.
8. Water when necessary. Tend to under-water, rather than over-water.
9. Look out for the rogues, sometimes known as Featherheads or Christmas trees. They have a dwarf, leafy appearance, and shorter inter-nodes, as well as many more side shoots. Directly these are seen in their baby stage, destroy them.

Preparation of the Site

Any ordinary soil will grow tomatoes, providing it is properly prepared. The heavy clays need opening up, and they had better be dug in the autumn and the land left rough so that the frost and cold winds may act on it and this will help to pulverise the clods. Heavy land can always be improved by working in plenty of bulky organic matter such as strawy manure, half-rotted vegetable refuse or even chopped straw. Light sandy soil that dries out quickly, can be improved by incorporating plenty of moisture-holding material, such as properly composted and fully rotted vegetable matter, or, of course, really well-rotted dung. Such material should be dug in about a spade's depth and, in addition, sedge peat may be forked into the top 2 or 3 inches when the ground is being prepared in the spring. You need about a bucketful per square yard, and in the case of clay soils the peat may be put on dry; with light sandy soils it should always be applied after it has been thoroughly soaked with water.

DRAINING THE LAND

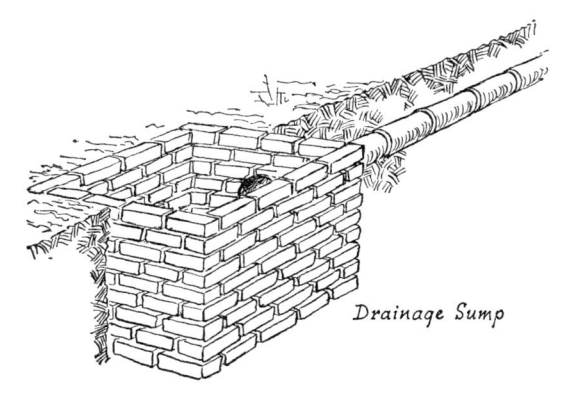

A Sump in the corner of the garden for the drainage water.

Light soils are usually low in potash and when obtainable, wood ashes should be applied at 6 to 8 ounces to the square yard. There are proprietary flue dusts on the market that can be used as a substitute at 5 ounces to the square yard. In addition, of course, care will be taken to use a liquid manure rich in potash – during the summer.

Heavy soils are often lacking in lime and an application of hydrated lime at 5 to 6 ounces per square yard will help to open them up. Lime should be given as a top dressing after the soil is prepared. Actually, there are light soils like those on Bagshot Sands which are deficient in lime.

Drains and Drainage

Trouble is often caused in private gardens because the soil is badly drained. This is sometimes because the original agricultural drains put down by the farmer were broken by the builder when the house was erected, so test the soil in the winter. Dig a hole 18 inches deep and if it soon fills with water you must suspect bad drainage, and you must do everything you can to remedy it. It is often possible to dig a trench a spade's width and 18 inches deep down the centre of the vegetable garden and fill this trench up with old brickbats, stones, clinkers, tins, etc., to a depth of 8 inches or so, with the object of ensuring ease of water movement. The surplus soil moisture will then travel down this drain which may, of course, be filled in once all the brickbats and the rubble are in position.

At the bottom of the garden a convenient square sump 3 feet wide can be dug and lined with bricks or breeze blocks and this can act as a kind of well. The water from the drain will fill it and having thus been collected, as it were, on the spot, it can be used in the summer if necessary for watering. The drains should be laid in the direction of the greatest slope.

Subsoil Watering

If, when digging over the land in the autumn, it is found that the subsoil is dry, it is worthwhile flooding the land as the digging proceeds. A hose should be used for the purpose so that as the digging proceeds, each 'trench' should be filled with water that must be allowed to soak through to the subsoil before the next spit is dug over. Generally speaking, it is more important to get the subsoil more thoroughly moist than the surface soil. Of course, in very wet winters or when there is much snow about, this subsoil flooding is not necessary.

The flooding should always be done after the organic matter has been dug in, but before the John Innes compost is put on the top. Often, after that it is necessary to water the plants when they are put in. This is usually known as ball watering.

Choosing the Site for Cloches

It is always advisable to choose a sunny position sheltered from the north and east winds. Cloches can conserve sun, but they cannot manufacture it. As has already been suggested, a south border is excellent, particularly one with a good wall or fence at the back from which reflected warmth can come. Such borders are always very dry and trench flooding should certainly be carried out, plus the digging-in of well-rotted organic matter. Tomatoes are sub-tropical plants and they do indeed revel in sunny positions. In allotments and gardens that have no such border, the rows are planted running north and south in a convenient place.

Choosing the Plants
Always choose sturdy, short-jointed, dark green plants. Never buy those long, lanky, yellowish, half-starved plants so often seen in shops. A short-jointed plant with nice dark green leaves is the one to go for, or produce yourself. See that it is true to type, however, and doesn't have too many side shoots. Water the plants the day before they are to be put out, so that the foliage will be firm and turgid. Plants from pots usually give the best results, especially those in paper, peat or compressed soil pots, for in these cases the pot and all are planted and there is no disturbance of roots. It isn't long before the peat or paper rots away and the roots by then are acclimatised to the temperature outside and are growing well. When plants are raised in clay pots, it is a good plan to put the plants in the hole, pot and all, for two or three days before knocking the ball of soil out of the pot and putting it into the ground. By then the temperature of the soil and the ground should be approximately equal.

Trenches and Planting
It has already been suggested that it is convenient to plant in trenches, so as to give extra height to the cloches, but this, of course, makes watering much easier to do also. Not only is it a simple matter to flood the trench but it is equally simple to feed with liquid manure. Again I emphasise that the trench must be 6 inches narrower at the top than the spread of the cloches and that the side must slope inwards to prevent the earth falling in.

Of course, the soil at the bottom of the trench will be made as near the John Innes Potting Compost No. 2 as possible, or if this is not convenient, ten days before planting, a compounded fish manure will be applied at 3 to 4 ounces to the yard run and lightly raked in, while on top of the ground will be sprinkled hydrated lime at, say, 16 ounces to the yard run.

N.B. – Where wireworms abound, it is worthwhile using an Aldrin dust worked into the top few inches. Try and buy the preparation which leaves no taint on root crops.

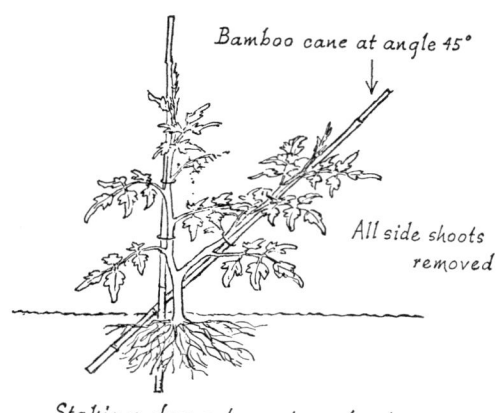

Bamboo cane at angle 45°

All side shoots removed

Staking for a two-stem plant

Tomato training.

Plant either on the flat or in the trench in such a manner that the plant is in with its lowest leaves at soil level. Handle the plants so that the stems are not squeezed or pinched. Rough handling kills more plants every year than is realised. Knock the plants out of the pots carefully (or if in paper, peat or compressed soil, plant pots and all), remove the crocks below the ball of soil, and insert the fingers at the bottom to spread out the roots a little. See that the soil is pressed down firmly around the roots but not around the stem. Try and leave a little depression around each plant for watering afterwards. Ball watering, as this is called, is important during the first week after planting. You see, it is necessary to keep the original ball of soil moist till the roots get through into the bulk of the soil around.

Methods of Staking

There are various ways of staking plants to be grown under cloches.

(1) This allows for the double-stem method of growing. Two bamboos or strong stakes are required for each plant, one being pushed in vertically, and the other at an angle of 45 degrees. The top of the diagonal stake is then tied to the top of the next vertical stake, as will be seen in the diagram opposite. The tops of the stakes should be arranged in such a manner that they are just below the centre of the top panes. The bottom side growth of each plant is then allowed to develop, being tied to the vertical stem, and the original main stem is tied to the diagonal stake. Naturally, when you use taller Ganwicks you

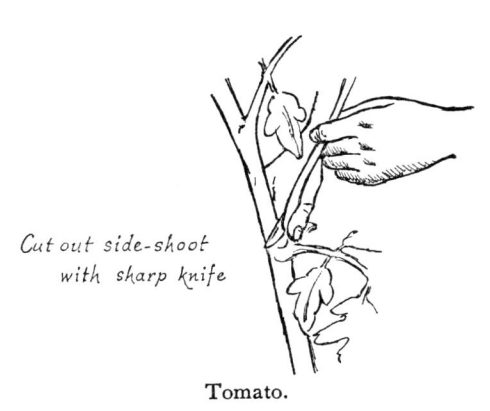

Cut out side-shoot with sharp knife

Tomato.

can have longer stakes than when you grow under dwarfer Ganwicks. When the plants reach the top of the stakes, the growing point of the stems must be pinched out.

(2) Insert two stout stakes at each end of the trench or tomato row. Drive them well into the ground because they will eventually have to support a great weight. Stretch a wire tightly between them so that it runs 2 inches below the tops of the Ganwicks to be used. Then insert a short bamboo for each plant and tie this firmly to the wire. The tomato plant should then be trained first of all up the stake and then carefully bent around and trained along the wire.

(3) Drive in posts as advised in Scheme 2, and stretch the

G*

wire tightly in a similar manner. Tie a length of string or 3-ply fillis to the wire at every point below which a tomato plant is set. Tie the bottom end of the string or fillis around the base of the plant with a loop to allow the stem to swell. You must not make a tight knot around the stem or else, as the plant grows, the string will cut into it. There is no need for the string to be absolutely taut, for as the plant grows it will be twisted around the string. When the plant gets to the top of the string it should be trained along the wire as advised in Scheme 2.

(4) Start the plants off under the cloches without any bamboo or support at all. Remove the top glass immediately all fear of frost has passed, say, at the beginning of June, and then give each plant an individual bamboo 5 feet long, or adopt the string and wire method as advised previously.

(5) Grow the plants on the flat under low cloches, but stop them at the leaf beyond the second truss, thus, only two trusses per plant. In this case, the tomatoes may be as close as 1 foot or 18 inches apart. No support need be given and because the plants are much closer together, an early heavier crop can be assured.

Side Shoot Removal

When they are allowed to grow naturally, tomatoes develop a large number of side shoots. These will be seen growing in the axils of the leaves. They should be removed carefully so as not to injure the flower trusses. The work has to be done once a week during the summer, the best method being to cut them out cleanly at their base with the tip of a sharp-bladed knife. The removal of the side growths should always be done when they are just under 1 inch long. Of course, when adopting the double stem system, as advised, one side shoot should be left at the base of each plant.

It is during this process that virus diseases are often transmitted, especially on the hands of smokers, for even after tobacco has been 'cured' there are American virus diseases which will go on living quite happily in the pipe, cigarette or cigar tobacco. No smoking, therefore, should be done when working among tomatoes and smokers should take every precaution to wash their hands in strong disinfectant and free them from any sign of stain. If the blade of a knife is used, this should be sterilised in formaldehyde first and if any of the plants are showing signs of trouble, it is better to dip the blade in a little jar of Formalin after working on even a slightly infected plant before working on another.

Defoliation

It is the leaves of the plant that manufacture the elaborated sap containing the 'sugars' that feed the fruits. Never, therefore, remove any leaves until absolutely necessary. Cut off the leaves when they turn yellow and when the fruit starts to ripen in the summer, cut off some of the foliage if it is very thick. Do not just remove the leaves at random. Cut off a whole leaf or two right at the base. To make certain that Botrytis (a fungus disease) does not spread, rub the cut end of the wound with a piece of 'Liver of sulphur'. At the end of the season when all the fruit has set, and all the leaves have done their bit, they may be cut off if, by doing so, ripening may be accelerated.

The exception is, of course, the badly diseased leaves which should always be cut away and put on the compost heap to rot down, immediately they are seen. Try, on the other hand, to prevent disease, by growing plants in ground rich in humus and, if necessary, by adopting preventative sprayings or dustings.

Tying Up the Plants

Tie the plants up to the stakes as they grow, each tie being made immediately above the leaf. Wrap the raffia, 3-ply fillis or string that you use, once round the bamboo or wire and then around the stem with a long loop, large enough to allow for natural expansion. Some firms sell split wire rings which are slipped round the bamboos and the plants immediately above each leaf, and time is saved. The split rings, of course, last several years and, therefore, are not expensive. It is necessary to make a tie every six inches up the plants or at every leaf.

In the case of the string support method, it is only necessary to twist the string around the plant and the right support is given by this spiral method.

Summer Feeding

Despite the fact that adequate organic matter has been dug into the ground when preparing the soil, and what is called a good 'base manure' of an organic character has been applied, it is necessary to give extra feeds from the time the bottom truss has set. Some people like to apply a dry fertiliser like fish manure around each plant and then water this in. Others prefer to use a liquid manure with an organic base.

It is a good plan to apply a half-strength Marinure feed after each flower truss sets, giving about $\frac{1}{2}$ gallon of this diluted manure per plant. Feeding should cease after the top truss is ripening well, and it is a good plan, therefore, to give one more feed after the setting of the top truss, say, a fortnight later.

Feeding must always be done intelligently, and if Bio-Humus is used, the type prepared for tomatoes should always be applied because it contains a high percentage of potash. There is no reason to continue giving liquid manure if the plants are growing too strongly, or appear to be too 'lush'. It is seldom, however, with a balanced feed that this occurs. However, should too much nitrogen have been given it may be toned down by the use of wood ashes at 7 ounces to the yard run.

Taking it by and large, you need more potash in a wet summer, and less in a dry, sunny season.

Watering and Mulching

It is always better to soak the ground around tomatoes than to apply a little sprinkling. Aim to do this flooding after each truss has set. Do not allow the soil to get dry. Many blossoms drop each year unfertilised because of the dryness at the roots. The digging in of organic matter to the soil to hold moisture when preparing the ground helps to provide a spongy reservoir.

Apply lawn mowings, water-soaked sedge peat, rotted leaves, or similar material, along the surface of the ground alongside the tomato rows to act as a mulch.

When growing the plants in trenches, the mulch can, of course, be put along the bottom. This top dressing has two functions: (a) it prevents the soil from splashing on the lower fruits when watering, and these soil splashes are often the cause of Buck-Eye Rot and (b) it helps to keep the moisture in down below by preventing surface evaporation. These mulches that help to keep the roots cool are gradually pulled into the ground by worms and there, of course, they continue to rot down and so help to provide extra humus.

Pollination and Fertilisation

Pollinating insects love to get under the cloches or Access frames and do the necessary work. They like to be out of the wind and appreciate the warmth. Therefore, on the whole, pollination is more satisfactory under cloches than in the open.

It is a good plan to syringe the plants over during the middle of the day with tepid water. Stand a bucket of water close to the cloches early in the morning so that it is at the right temperature when used at midday. The damp atmosphere that the spraying produces under the cloches helps to cause the pollen to germinate properly and the impact of the spray shakes the plants and so helps in distributing the pollen. Don't mind using plenty of force. It is quite easy to remove a top pane every now and then to enable the syringe, or better still, a Solo sprayer, with a long lance, to be used among the plants. When a Solo is used, it is seldom necessary to move more than every sixth pane.

Top Dressings

Tomato plants quite like sending out adventitious roots from the sides of their stems and when a new set of young vigorous roots do develop after the plants are half grown, fresh cropping zeal is implanted. Mulch, as advised in an earlier note, during the first week of June and then cover the mulching during the first week of July with a 2 - 3 inch depth of soil, mixed with an equal proportion of fine sedge peat, damped well first. New roots will grow into this and the plants will benefit accordingly.

Cloches for Ripening

Plants can be restricted by stopping; by pinching out the growing point, it is possible to keep the plants just the right size and then the cloches or access frames act as miniature greenhouses. Very often the tops of the cloches are removed to allow the plants to grow quite tall and then they are used again at the end of September to assist with ripening. In the north, protection may be necessary about the end of the third week of September.

The scheme is to cut the plants down from their stakes or string supports and then, having spread plenty of sedge peat or dry straw on the soil first, to lay the plants down on this. A certain number of the leaves that face towards the ground as the plants are laid down are cut off, and the tomato plants

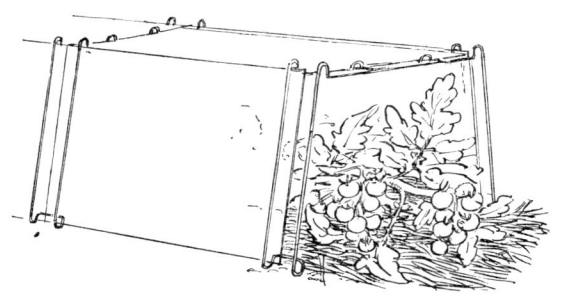

Ripening tomatoes under Ganwicks
Note the glass sides.

which are now lying on the peat or straw are covered with z cloches as in the diagram. The plants are thus protected from the frost and the fruits ripen perfectly. I have found it possible to pick ripe tomatoes from under cloches well on into the middle of November. See diagram above.

Discussing Varieties

How difficult it is to choose tomato varieties for somebody else. I quite like a large fruit. It should be firm with plenty of flesh. I dislike a small over-juicy tomato. I have known people however, who prefer a fruit that has got plenty of 'water' about it. Then there is the question of taste. I prefer the flavour of a variety like Histon Cropper to that of Ronaclave, but again it is a matter of opinion.

In trials I have carried out in various parts of the country I have found that the same variety can taste differently from one nursery to another. Soil, climate, aspect, different methods of feeding, and manuring can all play their part. Don't, therefore, be put off your pet variety by hearing someone else decry it. Do not, on the other hand, be so conservative that you are not willing to try another variety. My advice would be to stick to the variety you do know and like, but always try one or two of the new varieties each year to see if they are any improvement.

Ganwicks are now difficult to obtain and so at the experimental gardens of The Good Gardeners Association we have turned to Access Frames – these are very suitable.

CHAPTER XVIII

TOMATOES AND RING CULTURE

It is perhaps best to describe Ring Culture as Two Zone culture for the gardener aims to have 1 layer or zone of roots in a container and a second layer or zone of roots in some permeable material like sand or coarse ashes below. The idea then is to feed the upper layer of the roots regularly (which should be more fibrous), and to allow the lower layer of roots to convey the bulk of the moisture to the plant with little or no plant foods. The tomatoes are therefore grown in a whale hide bottomless pot or a similar container.

Ring culture, therefore, enables a gardener to grow an excellent crop of tomatoes without having any great depth of soil. Under this method a man can grow a heavy crop, say, above a gravel path, or on an ash bed. Most people who have adopted ring culture, have done so in the greenhouse. It means that a great bulk of the feeding roots can be controlled and supplied with plant foods in a nice warm container sitting on the surface of the soil, while the anchorage roots or water roots, as they are sometimes called, seek the moisture which the gardener supplies to the aggregate where, because of the openness of the material, there is plenty of aeration. One of the problems which faces the tomato-grower is keeping up the production once the first two trusses have set. Those who advocate ring culture claim that you get far better middle and upper trusses from this method than from growing the plants in soil.

Actually, the author does not practice this method now, though he did try it out for two or three years in the early stages – i.e. when the idea was first introduced. He contends that those who advocate this method of culture, do so because they have been disappointed in their soil, owing to the fact that they have neglected to apply properly composted vegetable waste regularly. It is when you build up the humus content of the soil faithfully, year after year, that it gets better and better, and when this happens, soil diseases are reduced to a minimum, worms are increased, and the plant roots are able to perform their normal function, without any trouble at all. However, as so many soils are crying out for humus today owing to having been neglected in the past, it may be as well for some readers to adopt ring culture until they've got their greenhouse and garden soils into the right condition – in some cases, this may take years.

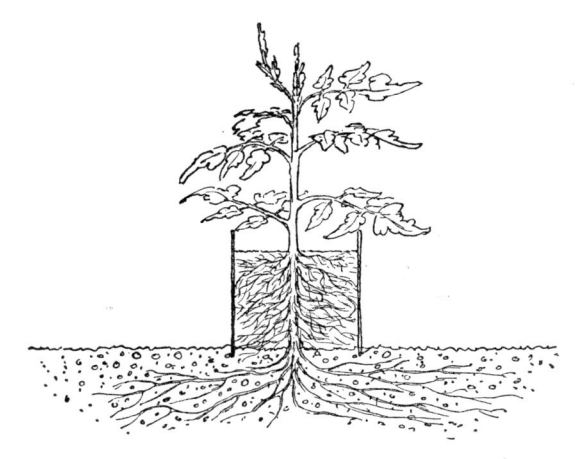

A Tomato growing in a bottomless pot – with the roots growing into the aggregate below.

The Ring Culture Container

Get hold of a number of whale hide pots with no bottoms to them, or use 8 or 10-inch pots with the bottoms knocked out. Bottomless boxes are a possibility, but whatever the container used, it should be capable of holding 14 lb. of compost. These bottomless containers, whatever they may be, are stood side by side on the aggregate, the tops being supported either by bamboos or string as described in Chapter XVI.

The Aggregate or Base

If it is necessary to fill the pots with compost before they are put on the aggregate, then a temporary bottom to the pots must be provided by using a square of wood or asbestos sheet; the pot can then be lifted on this and when it is put into its permanent position, the tile or square of wood is slipped out leaving the bottomless container sitting evenly on the aggregate.

Remembering that the scheme is to have the water in the lower zone, the material used must be highly water absorbent and yet really porous and open. The most suitable material is probably cinders and clinkers. As this is usually a waste product, it isn't too expensive. Before being used it must be well washed because it may contain some sulphur compounds which will cause trouble later on. Some gardeners use a mixture of washed gravel and coarse sand, the latter being very coarse, while others have put down a layer of coarse sedge peat to a depth of 1 foot or so, the bottomless pots being stood on this.

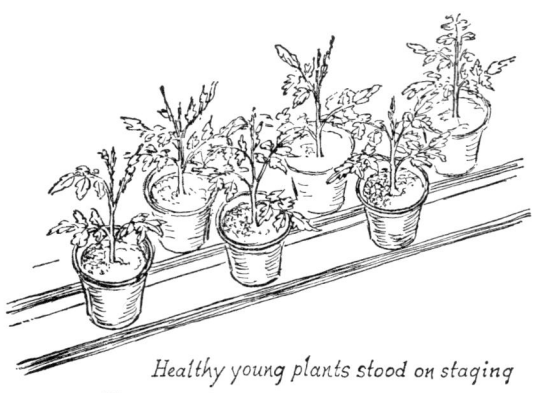

Healthy young plants stood on staging
Tomato plants being grown on.

Whatever the material used, it must never get waterlogged, for in this condition, it would be airless, and it must be a type of material that doesn't contain any plant foods at all. Personally, I don't like gravel because it doesn't hold the water sufficiently well, and the trouble with sedge peat is that after a time it tends to be compressed, and when that happens the air is driven out. All the aggregates used must, of course, be free from fungus disease and insect pests – that is to say, quite sterile. If broken clinkers and cinders are used, they should be put down to a depth of 4 to 6 inches in the greenhouse; the idea is to cover the whole of the floor, but out of doors where the plants are to be grown against a fence, for instance, a strip 18 inches wide and 4 inches deep will do. Some people dig out a trench of this width and depth and then fill it up with the broken clinkers. Once the pots are standing on the zone of water absorbent material, it should be arranged that the aggregate is kept moist from the beginning. It doesn't matter whether the planting is to be carried out towards the end of February in the greenhouse, in early April in a cold house, or in mid-May out of doors. Plenty of water is therefore given to the aggregate and hardly any water to the pots. Even in the hottest weather, the pots themselves will only require one pint of water each,

Potting tomato seedlings

Another stage of potting.

once a week. Though, in the middle of the droughty year of 1969, it was necessary to give a pint of water per plant twice a week.

Though the aggregate is drenched in order that the anchorage and water roots have what they need, a certain amount of moisture is, so to speak, sucked upwards in the compost, rather as ink rises up a piece of blotting-paper put in the ink pot. The pots themselves will be fed weekly with the correctly diluted Liquinure or some other organic liquid fertiliser like Marinure. The regular feeding may make the compost in the pots somewhat acid, and for this reason it's quite a good idea to give each pot 1 tablespoonful of carbonate of lime once every 4 weeks. This lime, having been distributed evenly over the top of the pot, should be washed in with a pint of water. The compost used in the pots should either be John Innes No. 2, or the Alex 'No-Soil' Compost, with the necessary plant foods supplied by the vendors in a plastic bag.

When clay pots are used or even cement pots, these are extremely porous and moisture is evaporated from the sides of the pots as a result. This means that watering has to be done between feeds, especially during the month of August, and early September, when the plants are heavily laden and the weather really hot. Always give pots light applications of water if they need it, but the aggregate a regular flooding. To give an idea of the amount of water that is used per 12 plants in the aggregate, I would say that in 1969, 4 gallons were needed every day.

Extraordinary weights of plants have been produced under this particular method of culture, i.e. 10 lb. per plant, 12 lb. per plant, and in one case as much as 20 lb. per plant – these figures, of course, being under glass and in quite tall houses where the plants could grow upwards undisturbed. In all these cases, liquid fertilisers were used every week or ten days in accordance with the instructions on the containers. One uses a liquid food with a high potash content when the weather is dull and rainy, and liquid manure with a high nitrogen content when the weather is sunny and when the plants are heavy with fruit.

Firming soil in pot with finger-tips

The Tomato seedling being potted-up in its right stage.

CHAPTER XIX

A FEW SIMPLE RECIPES

In the chapters dealing with the various vegetables and salads some attempt has been made to suggest how they may best be used. Salad making is undoubtedly an art, but it is an art that can be learned – and learned, too, by practice. Again may I say, at the risk of repeating myself, please don't be conservative. Be willing to try something new, and as a result you will find that there are a multitudinous number of flavours which can turn what might be an ordinary salad into something quite out of the ordinary.

The chapter on herbs says something of the purslane which somehow adds a nutty taste to the salad; there are the mints which seem to add a coolness; there is the delicious lemon flavour of the balm. Don't overdo these herbs in a salad or they will dominate the whole bowl and this is a mistake. For instance, it is quite enough to wipe a clove or two of garlic around a bowl before putting the salad in, in order to get just the right flavouring of garlic. Aim at getting suspicions of flavours and you will find that your household will love the salads which you make.

Then try different combinations. Brussels sprouts, turnip tops and grated carrots, or beetroot tops, grated Hamburg parsley roots, chopped celery and some grated cauliflower. Yet another might be lettuce, tomato, cucumber, some fresh peas, together with some grated swede and onion. All the vegetables mentioned in this book can be used as salads and you will be able to work out recipes of your own. You will use those vegetables that come in together, and that are available together.

Don't forget, too, that in these salads you can put, as they come in season, sliced or grated portions of apple, or of pear, or if you have dried your plums, you will be able to have sliced prunes in the salad – and your own prunes too! You may have a walnut tree and be able to add your own walnuts, or a cob-nut tree from which you can pick your own cob-nuts and filberts, or even an almond tree which will produce your almonds for 'roasting'!

In the Elizabethan days, flowers and flower petals were used far more than they are now. Have you ever thought of brightening up a salad by sprinkling over the top of the salad bowl petals from some of the edible flowers? There is nothing wrong in eating flowers. In fact, many people say it is much better to eat them than to have them in your buttonhole and let them die. If they suffer at all they suffer far more that way. The following flowers are quite edible : – marigolds, nasturtiums, anchusa, rosemary, lavender, sage, roses, bergamot, borage, and Virginian stock. Our great grandmothers used to say that marigold flowers were particularly useful, for they were so health-giving.

THESE ARE SO GOOD

It isn't just a crank's idea that we should eat more salad or even that we should eat more vegetables. It is the leading dietitians who say that our planned food programme should consist of only 25 per cent of proteins and starches, i.e. the meat, bread, cheese, eggs, cakes, and most puddings, and 75 per cent of vegetables and fruits which produce the necessary alkalis, for the proteins and starches are certainly acid forming. This means that most of us are having unbalanced rations, and if the war of 1939-1945 has done any good, it is to reduce the amount of meat, etc. which it is possible to buy.

This book aims at getting men and women to eat more vegetables raw, for thus are vegetables of the greatest value to the human race. Take the dandelion, for instance, which is so much despised. It contains four times as much Vitamin C as lettuce, and more iron than almost any other vegetable. Parsley, as already recommended, is very rich in Vitamin A and is as good, therefore, as a dose of Cod Liver Oil, while its Vitamin C content is three times richer than oranges which before the 1939 war used to be thought ideal for children.

The root crops when grated and served raw are so easily digested. Turnips, for instance, contain sulphur, which helps with many ills. Cook the turnips and the content of sulphur may make it indigestible. When you grate carrots and eat them raw, you find them to be rich in iron, lime, magnesium, and potash, and the same holds good for parsnips, radishes, etc.

If you are going to make the best salad, cut the plant you are going to eat as short a time as possible before you put it into the salad bowl. Don't cut early in the morning and then not serve until lunch time. That is the great advantage of growing your own vegetables, and the man in the town who has no garden, can never have a good salad. Don't leave salads in a lot of water for hours at a time or they get soft and flabby, and don't forget that you should never bruise the leaf of any plant that you are going to use for a salad or even crush it. The French know the secret of this, because they always dry their lettuces, endive, and corn salad, by swinging them round and round in the air, tied up in butter muslin or placed in a wire basket.

Don't mix up the salad in the kitchen an hour or two before you are going to serve it. If you are going to serve the salad with a dressing, put the latter in the bottom of the bowl first of all, and carefully arrange the ingredients of the salad on top. Then just before serving, mix the salad up together with bone or imitation bone salad servers, sprinkling with a little sugar or pepper and salt to taste. If flowers are to be put on, these should be added last, for if they are mixed in with the dressing, they, of course, lose their bright colour.

Chicory

Slice the chicory leaves up finely, and serve with winter lettuce or endive. Mix in some chopped parsley, or as an alternative, winter savory. A little horse-radish stirred in makes an interesting change.

Cabbage

Should be shredded. Chopped up celery goes well with it, as also do tiny radishes. It is interesting to serve such salad in an upfolded cup-shaped cabbage leaf.

Celery

Can well be served alone, or chopped and mixed with cucumber and red radishes. It is possible also to pull off the rounded stems carefully and fill these up or stuff them with some soft cheese. They are then served separately and look most attractive if displayed in a bowl. Celery also goes well with nuts and with parsley.

A good salad can be made with celery, grated turnips, and grated carrots, mixed with a little chopped chives and chopped parsley and decorated with some chervil.

Cucumber

If the cucumber can be cut up thinly enough it need not be peeled, and it can then be served alone or put on as a top dressing, so to speak, over any other salad mixture. Another way is to cut the cucumber into squares and to cut an equal quantity of melon into squares also. Some mint should then be chopped up and added to the salad, and if possible a little tarragon also. A little sugar should be sprinkled over the top. Nasturtium flowers and leaves go well with cucumber also.

Endive

Endive mixes well with watercress or ordinary cress, chopped celery and grated turnip. In the autumn it goes well with sliced apple. People who find endive a little bitter will like it when other vegetables and salad plants are mixed in with it.

Mustard and Cress

You always need about twice the amount of cress to mustard, and if you want an interesting salad bowl, mix a little finely chopped apple in, and decorate the bowl with rose petals or nasturtium petals.

CHAPTER XX

SEED SAVING AND TOMATOES

SOME gardeners like to save their own tomato seed year after year and many have done this with great success. Very often better and quicker germination is obtained from home-saved seed, especially when the saving is done from healthy, sturdy plants. The great thing is to start thinking about saving seeds early in the season and to mark down a plant or plants which have all the right characteristics. The fruits should be of the desired shape. The leaves should be of the right space apart. The plants should be strong and sturdy. There should be no signs of disease or of virus trouble. These perfect plants should be watched. If one or more of them show signs of deterioration, the coloured stakes should be removed.

It is asserted that the best seed comes from the four fruits nearest the main stem of the plant, on the third or fourth truss. These fruits should be allowed to remain on the plants until they become soft through over-ripeness. They should then be picked and placed in a shallow box to complete the ripening process. Do not remove the seeds until the fruits are thoroughly ripe.

When completely ripe, open the fruits and put the pulp and the seeds in clean water in a vessel which can be kept at a temperature of about 65 degrees F. Fermentation takes place within 48 hours, and all that has to be done is to remove the scum floating from the top of the vessel and to drain off the liquid. The seeds are then tipped out, washed, and placed on sheets of blotting-paper or newspaper to dry.

Put the sheets containing the seeds in a warm room and within 48 hours the seeds may be loosened from the paper and mixed with a little silver sand. Rub the seed and the sand together through the hands, and so give the coats of the seeds a clean finish. Separate any seeds that may have stuck together. Sieve through a household sieve to get rid of the sand, and packet the seeds and put away properly labelled.

Another method is known as the soda method; $\frac{1}{4}$ lb. of soda is dissolved in 1 quart of water and an equal amount of pulp is added, the whole being heated to a temperature of 68 degrees F. In about 4 to 8 hours, the seeds will be ready to clean and dry out. If you soak the pulp and heat to a temperature of 140 degrees F. the whole process only takes about 10 minutes and the seed can be dried off as in the method already described.

Those who propose to save their own seeds should know that from 3 lb. of good fruit, it is possible to obtain $\frac{1}{4}$ ounce of excellent tomato seed; $\frac{1}{4}$ ounce of good seed should produce 1,500 plants. Thus it will be seen that there should be very little difficulty for any keen grower to save his own seed, and in fact, it is possible to improve the strain year after year.

APPENDIX

What the No-Soil Compost Really Is

The No-Soil Compost is a complete Seedling Potting Compost. It is basically composed of sedge peat and sand with lime and fertiliser additions, and as the name implies, it contains no soil or loam at all. Owing to the difficulty of obtaining suitable potting soil for traditional potting composts and the variable results often experienced by using indifferent soils or loams, the No-Soil Compost offers a standard growing medium for all types of plants.

The sedge peat used is specially chosen for its structural strength, as the physical properties of the compost have to remain good for a very long time, perhaps for several years, in the case of a conservatory or stove house plant, also sedge peat has a high colloidal content which is very essential for the holding and release of plant nutrients. In this respect the sedge peat does the work of the clay in a soil.

The grading or particle size of the peat has been carefully designed to reduce drying out to a minimum and ensure maximum water retention with adequate air space. The grading and type of sand has been specially selected for the purpose.

The No-Soil Compost is a dual purpose compost. It can be used for both seed sowing and potting-on. When supplied, the main bulk is Seed Compost and this contains lime and an adequate amount of plant nutrients for the early development of the seedling. Within each bag of Seedling Compost is a sachet of Potting Base. The Seedling Compost is converted into Potting Compost by the addition of the Potting Base. Depending on the strength of the Potting Compost required, Potting Composts Nos. 1, 2 or 3 can be made up by adding 11 ounces, 22 ounces, or 33 ounces of Potting Base per bushel respectively. The Potting Base should be thoroughly mixed with the Compost. There is sufficient Potting Base in the sachet to convert the whole of the Seedling Compost in the pack to Potting Compost No. 3 if required.

For seed raising generally, the Seedling Compost alone may be used. If it is intended that the seedlings are to remain in the seed tray for some time after germination, i.e. with space sowing or with very slow-growing subjects, Potting Compost No. 1 should be used. Where, for insance, strong-growing plants such as brassicas are to be raised in peat pots, by sowing 2 or 3 seeds per pot and thinning to one and growing-on, to avoid pricking off, Potting Compost No. 3 is suggested.

For Bedding plants and potting-on work in the spring, No. 3 compost is recommended. Potting Compost No. 2 should be used for very delicate subjects or for plants which are intended to be potted-on again fairly soon. In the autumn, young plants should be pricked off into No. 2, but well established plants being potted-on, into No. 3.

In using the No-Soil Compost, it is important to appreciate that the compost should be conditioned with 10 pints of water per bushel before use. In the case of Potting Compost, the Potting Base must be added and thoroughly mixed in before the compost is wetted up. When potting, do not over-firm but give a good first watering to settle the compost. Leave adequate watering space at the top of the pot so that sufficient water may be added at one time to completely wet the compost in the pot, bearing in mind that the 'No-Soil' Compost will hold three times more water than a traditional loam. Also because of this, avoid over-watering in the early stages of plant growth and during dull periods. Should the Compost accidentally dry out during use, it must be reconditioned with two good waterings, or the pot stood in shallow water.

Owing to the very free root run and the capacity of the compost to hold nutrients, larger plants are usually produced and earlier spacing out may be required.